The People's H

The Bonny Fisher Lad

Memories of the North Northumberland Fishing Community

Edited by

Katrina Porteous

Craster looking west, circa 1900, before the harbour was built. The cottages of Dunstanburgh Road have not yet been enlarged. Hens peck around their doors and the ruins of earlier cottages lie in front of them.

Previous page: Left to right: William 'Pat' Laidler, Andrew Rutter and Bob Rutter, Seahouses, circa 1930.

First published in 2003 by

The People's History Ltd
Suite 1, Byron House
Seaham Grange Business Park
Seaham, Co. Durham
SR7 0PY

ISBN 1 902527 48 8

Contents

Holy Islanders at work, early 1900s. The two women bait lines into a swull filled with grass to separate the rows.

The Bonny Fisher Lad

O the bonny fisher lad
That brings the fishes frae the sea,
O the bonny fisher lad,
The fisher lad gat haa'd o' me.

On Bamboroughshire's rocky shore,
Just as you enter Boulmer Raw,
There lives the bonny fisher lad,
The fisher lad that bangs them aa'.

O the bonny fisher lad
That brings the fishes frae the sea,
O the bonny fisher lad,
The fisher lad gat haa'd o' me.

My mother sent me out one day
To gather cockles frae the sea;
But I had not been lang away
When the fisher lad gat haa'd o' me.

O the bonny fisher lad
That brings the fishes frae the sea,
O the bonny fisher lad,
The fisher lad gat haa'd o' me.

A sailor I will never marry,
Nor soldier, for he's got no brass;
But I will have a fisher lad
Because I am a fisher lass.

O the bonny fisher lad
That brings the fishes frae the sea,
O the bonny fisher lad,
The fisher lad gat haa'd o' me.

Traditional

'Waiting for smacks, Craster.'

Introduction

This is a book about the fishing communities of north Northumberland. It includes the villages of Holy Island, Seahouses, Beadnell, Newton-by-the-Sea, Craster and Boulmer, all of which grew up around fishing. In this they differ from their neighbours, Bamburgh and Embleton, which are not included in this volume. The photographs and testimony record the changes which have taken place in these communities over the last century. Although history is a continuous process of change, fishing has suffered such a crisis in recent years that all six villages are now, to a greater or lesser extent, undergoing a profound shift in character.

In the distant past, the people of the north Northumberland coast were subsistence farmers and fishermen. Fishing gradually grew in economic importance, and industrial development – especially of the railways, by which fish could be transported swiftly to new markets – meant that, by the mid-19th century, fishing had become a major business.

Though each of the six villages retained its distinctive characteristics, all shared common features. For the women as much as for the men, fishing was more than a job: it was a way of life. Because of this, the six villages had in many ways more in common with Burnmouth on the Scottish coast, or with Staithes in Yorkshire, than with villages four or five miles inland. All followed a similar annual pattern, fishing for crabs in the spring, herring in summer, and for white fish using long lines in winter. Some, like Seahouses, Beadnell and later Craster, had harbours. But this was not necessary to an industry based on the traditional Northumbrian boat, the coble. The harbours were built to serve other industries: quarrying, lime-burning and grain production, all of which were important to the six villages at different times.

I have depended upon the kindness of many families for the text and pictures in this book. The photographs are drawn entirely from private sources. Sixty of them were lent to me by the late Craster fisherman, Bill Smailes; more of his collection can be seen on the Sables-Smailes Bygone Craster website. Most of the postcards come from the collection of George Nairn ('Picture the Past'). Many Beadnell and Seahouses photographs were lent by David Horsley from the albums of his late father, Tom. Others come from my own grandfather's collection, and from individuals, including: John and Kathleen Dixon, Charlie Douglas, May Douglas, Pauline Moore, Catherine Petty, Andrew Rutter and others. Although every effort has been made to acknowledge the source of photographs, inevitably some exist in multiple copies and original provenance may be doubtful. If I have infringed copyright in any instance, I can only offer my sincere apologies.

The text is based on two sources: first, interviews recorded on tape over a 10–year period between 1989 and '99; and, secondly, a fascinating 140–page account of life as a fisherman, written by Bill Smailes. Most of the interviews were recorded between 1990 and '92. They span a generation: my oldest interviewee was born in 1894, my youngest in 1920. Three were women, eleven men. This was a generation which valued memory. The men in particular relied on their memories for their livelihood. They carried in their heads a map of the sea-floor that was as much cultural as geographical: they could remember who had caught what, where and in exactly what circumstances. Many of them related stories that their grandfathers had told them, stretching back to the 1850s or before. Several people who began as my interviewees became my close friends. Sadly, other work commitments made me slow to publish, and far too few of them have lived to see the completion of this book.

I recorded so many hours of interviews that only a tiny fraction is included here. These lives were so full, and the skills and knowledge involved in fishing so enormously detailed, that this book can only be a bare introduction. There are obvious omissions: not every family from each community has been represented or given due mention. Inevitably, as an incomer to the area and a landsman, I will have made other mistakes. For these I apologise. History is always a matter of debate and argument, never more so than in villages.

Reproducing both text and photographs has presented a challenge. If sometimes in the pictures the sea horizons look skewed, this is generally a problem with the original rather than with the layout or the reader's eyesight! As for the interviews, most of the transcriptions were in broad Northumbrian dialect, which varies from village to village, even from family to family. I have chosen to edit these to make them comprehensible to a wider audience. But where possible, I have retained some original grammar and included some dialect words. I have tried to steer a course between accessibility and respect for the speaker's individual voice. More obscure dialect and technical terms are explained in a glossary at the back of the book.

I am extremely grateful to everyone who read the typescript and offered corrections and advice, and to the Kathleen Blundell Trust and the Society of Authors for financial support which helped me to complete the book.

My admiration for every one of the people I interviewed is boundless. Theirs was a generation which saw more change than any other in history. They were born into a world without running water or electricity, some before the age of the motor car or the aeroplane, when boats were still powered by sail and oar. They lived through two World Wars, to witness the development of television, home computers, digital recording, antibiotics, contraceptive pills, jet air travel and thousands of other technological advances. In many ways, the industrial revolution came late to fishing; my interviewees saw the introduction of radar, Decca navigators, echo-sounders, global positioning satellites, and – in ports far from their own – 250 foot fishing boats the size of small hotels. And with them, they saw a way of life that was handed down for generations all but disappear.

Many of the villages featured here can scarcely call themselves fishing villages any more. They depend instead on the tourist industry. Ironically, tourists are drawn to working harbours, to the practical tradition and continuity which fishing embodies. Aware that their way of life is disappearing, the fisher people I interviewed look back unsentimentally to a time of hardship, of poverty; yet speak also, with humour and wisdom, of what we have lost. Their lives depended upon close bonds of family and community – not always easy – and upon their respect for the natural world. Every one of them knew that, in their lives, the sea was the boss, and that to survive and succeed they must cooperate with nature, not assume mastery over it. Technological developments have sometimes left us all blind to that message, with potentially disastrous consequences. In that sense, this tale of the decline of small-boat fishing is not just the story of a few Northumbrian villages: it is all our stories.

Katrina Porteous,
Beadnell 2003

Contributors

Holy Island

Robin Henderson (1910-1996) *RH*
Ralph Wilson (1919-2001) *RW*

Seahouses

Jimmy (1904-1992) and Rhoda (1906-1996) Walker *JW* and *RhW*
Tom Dawson (1910-1994) *TDw*
Andrew Rutter (1912-2000) *AR*
William 'Pat' Laidler (Born 1913) *PL*

Beadnell

Tom Douglas (1906-2001) *TD*
Charlie Douglas (1909-1995) *CD*
Maggie Fawcus (Mrs Georgina Fryer, born 1917) *MF*
Mrs May Douglas (Born 1920) *MD*

Craster

Jack Hall (1894-1991) *JH*
Bill Smailes (1920-2002) *BS*

Boulmer

George Stanton (Born 1911) *GS*

In addition, I have included contributions from George Livingston Shell (1911-1994) *LS* of Holy Island, in conversation with Andrew Rutter, and from Mrs Maisie Bell (1910-1998) *MB* of Beadnell.

Herring keelboats in Seahouses harbour, circa 1908. The Margaret Dawson BK 171 (foreground) was owned by a partnership of the Dawson family and skippered by George Dawson. She was the first Seahouses keelboat to have an engine.

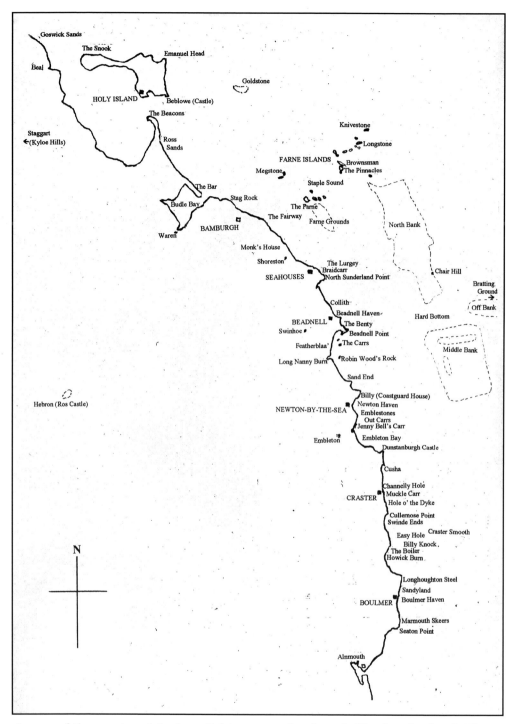

A map of the coast and inshore fishing grounds of north Northumberland. The scale is approximately one inch to three and a quarter miles.

THE VILLAGES

Conveyances for Hire.

Telegrams, R. Bell, Holy Island.

Crossing the Sands, Holy Island.

Crossing the sands, Holy Island, circa 1918. There was no paved road until 1954. Bob Bell the postmaster served for 46 years and was awarded the British Empire medal in 1953.

Holy Island

While the Christian history of Holy Island, or Lindisfarne, is well-known, much less has been written about its secular history – the lives of Islanders who, cut off by the tide twice daily, made their living from the land and sea. The lime industry prospered on the Island in the 18th and 19th centuries and, by the mid-19th century, herring fishing was booming. In 1841 Holy Island had 12 herring boats and 16 white-fishing boats; by 1863 it had 37 herring boats.

Holy Island, with its dozen or so inns, had a wild reputation for smugglers, drunken brawls and, in earlier times, wreckers, who were said to lure ships onto the rocks for plunder. However, it was also one of the first places in the country to have its own lifeboat.

The causeway, begun in 1954, was a symbol of the changing times, which have seen a once-isolated community become one of the most popular tourist attractions in the area. Piped water arrived in 1955 and electricity two years later. There are now only four shellfish boats fishing out of Holy Island, and one small trawler which works from other ports.

My interviewees were Robin Henderson of Lifeboat House and Ralph Wilson MBE of Manor House. Both men were Holy Island fishermen all their lives, and both served with distinction on the lifeboat.

Robin Henderson

The first boat I went in was the *Morning Light*. She'd be about 28 feet. I was fourteen and I detested the damn thing. I was sick for two years afore I got the better of it. I've looped the loop a few times since those days! After World War I, they started to get engines in them. My last boat was called the *Ocean Maid*.

There wouldn't be a tremendous lot of fishermen on the Island when I was young. There've always been nine or ten boats. They dress different now, young fishermen. The older people all wore blue jerseys or blue suits. Most of them had peaker-caps on – what ye call 'cheesecutters'.

The Ouse, Holy Island, circa 1905. A herring boat is moored in the bay and barrels are lined up against the herring houses. Richard Perry wrote that, in the 1860s, 'a man could walk on upturned herring barrels for half a mile from the great bricked curing house on the green above the Ouse to the castle jetty.'

When I was a youngster we respected three people: the schoolmaster, the nurse and the vicar. There's no respect these days.

It was a great place for sailors, Holy Island. There was always ships in. And there was about 22 taverns here, I would think. In the olden days it must have been a hell of a place. There's one thing now: ye never see anybody drunk, pallatic, like there used to be. I've seen them heels up in the street there. They couldn't stand.

A tourist card showing views of Holy Island, circa 1930, without a car in sight.

Ralph Wilson's Memories

There were at least nine pubs here. That would be about the time the quarry was working. There was a lot more people living on the Island at that time, and no more houses than there are now; probably less. So they must've lived mighty thick. And all had big families. They slept in the old box-beds. There were very few families that didn't have five or six in the family.

There was Tom Kyle; he was the Coxswain of the lifeboat, and a fisherman. He lived at the Castle Hotel. He was one of the characters at that time. He was Coxswain for a long time, followed by Johnny Markwell. Now there's no Markwells on the Island. That name's finished. There's one or two old names disappeared.

There were no steam drifters here. There were sailing drifters, and they all finished about the 1900s. They're the ones that are upturned on the beach there. The herring fishing was finished about the 1900s.

The Boat Sheds

I can remember the two big ones along at the north side – they've been there all my life, and I can remember 70 years. They're good condition, great big heavy keelboats. Herring boats, ye know. Then there are smaller ones. The boat we had before the *Morning Light*, the *Guiding Star*, she's on the beach as a boat-house now.

Then there's the *Sunshine*. She belonged old Geordie Cromarty, Coxswain of the lifeboat. I was 19 years old and I was away playing football. When I came back, my father and them had it upside down on the beach.

The one next to it came from Seahouses. Belonged Charlie Dawson's father. The *Providence*, they called that one. Aye, and they've called their boats *Providence* ever since.

There's one called the *Magpie*. Now the fella that owned that, he lost his life with the punt-gun. An accident, aye. And then there's the *Breadwinner*. That one was going to sea when I went. And there's one that came during World War I: *Elsie*, they call it. And there's the *Hope*. And the *Joan Keen*. That 'un came from Berwick.

RH

Ralph Wilson

I started going to sea when I was 14 and a half. The first two or three months after leaving school I gathered winkles – periwinkles. Then the man that went to sea with my father took ill and couldn't go back, so I had to go into the boat with him at 14 and a half.

The boat I started on, a coble, came from the Halls of Beadnell. Built in 1921, it was called the *Reliance*. I think it was too big for Beadnell, for pulling up. I think it would be in the region of £40. And it had a new engine put into it at Seahouses by Robson, a Kelvin engine, 12/14, and a new shaft into it – I remember that.

The sailing boats were finished when I started. Some of them carried a sail, but only for an emergency. I cannot remember anybody with a sail up, other than if he broke down. We had petrol-paraffin engines. Kelvin engines, most of them – they started up on petrol and ran on paraffin. It was a long time after the War before any diesels came on.

So I went away with my father to the potting and the line-fishing in the winter. Father pulled all by hand. He wasn't a big man, really, but he must have had terribly strong arms. Then I eventually made the first pot-hauler that it had in it. I made it myself with the old car gear-box and back-axle. And that was in the *Reliance* when we sold it. I've had one or two boats since then, but

Visitors to Holy Island, July 1939. The herring boats and herring houses are by this time long-disused, and some of the boats converted into sheds.

in the last few years I've semi-retired. I've just been paddling at the salmon-fishing here on my own. I didn't like the idea of stopping. The hardest job I have now is walking up from the beach with an oilskin under my arm and a pair of big sea-boots on!

I was on the Sea Fisheries Committee for 31 years. I was chairman for the last eight or nine years. Everybody'll tell ye – I always spoke out what I thought. When I had to finish, at 70, I got honoured by the Queen, so I must have done my service.

Oyster-keeper

My father's father, Ralph Wilson, was an oyster-keeper on the Beacons on Ross Links. He lived in that house between the Beacons for many years, as an oyster-keeper for Lord Tankerville who owned all that coastline. The whole family lived over there, and my father and the other brothers went to school from there. Some of them would be born over there, 'cos there were three girls as well as the three boys.

If Lord Tankerville wanted two dozen oysters at the weekend, they had to get into the horse and cart and take them up to Chillingham Castle. In the end it was made defunct. But they were there quite a long time.

They walked from the Beacons to Belford to school for two years; and then my grandfather got a small boat built at Lees of Berwick, a sailing boat, about 14 foot long, and they came over here to (Holy Island) school by boat. And they carried their water from here. There was a well over there, actually at the lifeboat station – they had a lifeboat station at Ross links – but it was locked up. So if it was bad weather and they couldn't get across to here and they ran short, they used to have to go and knock the padlock off to get the water!

I think they must have had a fairly rough life of it over there. My father came back and went to the fishing over here in the boat the *Jane*. Two or three years he had a fish-shop in Edinburgh; but we came back here when I was about five and a half or six, and I've been here ever since.

RW

Crossing the sands to Holy Island, circa 1927. Then, as now, it was unwise to leave it too late.

Seahouses

Over the last century and a half, Seahouses, originally known as North Sunderland, has been the biggest of the six fishing communities featured in this book. Its harbour was begun in 1786; huge quantities of lime and grain were shipped from here. From the middle of the 19th century, herring became a major export, and in 1856 North Sunderland had 51 resident herring and 12 white-fishing boats.

The harbour was extended in the 1880s. By 1889, 150 men and boys from the village were said to be directly employed in fishing. By this time up to 300 herring boats, from as far afield as the West Coast of Scotland and St Ives in Cornwall, put into North Sunderland harbour in summer. The present harbour was built to accommodate them. As many as ten curing yards operated in the village. Some writers claim that kippers were invented here by John Woodger in the mid-19th century.

With its larger harbour, North Sunderland was better able to cope with changes in fishing practices in the early 20th century than were some of the smaller communities; it continued to sustain a herring industry until the 1970s.

By this time there were still about 70 fishermen in Seahouses and nine salmon licences. Today there is no salmon fishing from Seahouses, no trawler permanently based there, and no working coble. Only a handful of crab and lobster boats and one smokehouse remain. The principal use of the harbour is now for 'party-boats' carrying visitors to the Farne Islands.

My interviewees from the village were: Jimmy and Rhoda Walker, a fisherman and his wife with nearly a century of lifeboat service between them; Tom Dawson MBE, RNLI Bronze Medal holder, and lifeboat Coxswain for 16 years; William 'Pat' Laidler, born in Eyemouth but a Seahouses fisherman all his life; and Andrew Rutter, who as well as being a fisherman was a skilled engineer, writer and gifted artist.

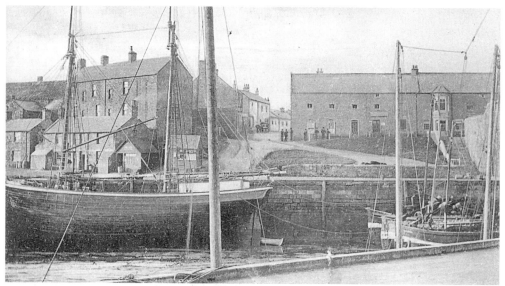

A schooner and herring boats, Seahouses harbour, early 1900s. Above the Bamburgh Castle Inn (right) was a school, then a reading room and doctor's surgery. The houses (left) were fishermen's cottages. Tom Dawson was born in the end house of the top row. Twenty-one children lived in this cottage and the next.

Tom Dawson

When I started, the motors were beginning to come in. My father had a large herring boat, and things were very, very poor. I started when I was 14 in the herring boat. The first summer I was there, we were £12 in debt. The next year, we were £18 in debt. Very difficult! We ate a lot of herring! – and potatoes. Tetties an' herrin'. One of your main meals.

The herring boats would be six a crew, but the ordinary fishing, it was three or four men, just about the same as it is now. See, most of the fishing boats are run by families. And they carry about three or four men. I don't believe in going any less than three. A lot of the boats nowadays are working one or two men, and I do not agree with that at all. It's far too dangerous. Well, if one man gets over the side, what's the other man going to do?

Changes are vast: different methods of fishing and one thing and another. We worked harder in those days for what we got, I think. But, nevertheless, families were happy. There was ten of us. We lived down at the harbour.

When I was first married – have ye ever been at Swallow's fish shop? Well, that's where I lived. We had a daughter and a son. And my son's at sea (1991). And my father was a fisherman, and his father before him. We've been connected with the sea for many, many years. We've had five *Providences* now.

Tom Dawson's Memories of Seahouses

Ye see, at one time, there wasn't any village here. North Sunderland was the village. And I don't know if you know the infants' school up there, on the Main Street? Well, that's the school I went to. Now, there's a gate just below that. Nowadays it goes up to the club. That gate was named the 'Fishers' Gate'. And the fishermen – when they were ashore, they never came below that gate, or very seldom. The reason for that was the Excise Men. Because, if the Excise Men landed, they had time to go all the way into the country to hide. They used to haul them into the Navy. Oh aye. Press gangs. It must have finished a long time ago, but that was the fact. Father used to tell us that.

The Press Gang

Beadnell village, like North Sunderland, is situated at some distance from the sea:

They used to say Charlie Steen's old grandfather, he was 'three times pressed.' That was why fishermen, olden days, lived up the country – Swinhoe and Shoreston and them places.

CD

Tom Dawson, second left, Seahouses harbour, August 1927. To his left is his brother, George 'Ginger' Dawson, and on his right are 'Buttony' Dawson and Tom and Ginger's father, Charlie Dawson.

Fishermen at Shoreston

When I was a laddie going to the school, the old'uns used to hand things down by word of mouth. And, of course, with the advent of modern civilisation all this has disappeared – there's a great loss. And my granny and my mother used to tell me there was fishermen at Shoreston. And they used to come down the Burn to Monk's House, and they kept their boats at Monk's House. Ye know when Shoreston went out of existence? In the latter 1400s. And people remembered all that time.

AR

North Street at the bottom of Dunstan View, Seahouses, early 1900s. G. Archbold's Cash Grocery Stores (centre right) was later a fish and chip shop. On the right side of the street, also at a later date, were two of the main shops in the village, Roper's and Rachel's.

Andrew Rutter's Memories

My great uncle was pilot here. He used to go aboard the ships – ye had to be a registered pilot then. He used to take them in, ye see, because probably the sailing ship wouldn't come into this port every time. So they were all strange waters for them, and the pilots used to bring them in to eliminate any error.

Now, when Sir Richard Terry was researching a book for the shanties, he was pally with old Lord Runciman that had Shoreston Hall. And they always used to come down to talk to my grandfather, because they were both old deep water men. I've seen the two of them sitting on top of the fire; old Runciman sitting yarning away – it was all rope and canvas and one thing and another; and me as a little boy, sitting between them with the lugs flapping. And he got my grandfather to sing some of the shanties, and they're in Richard Terry's book. So there ye are!

The house I was born in was next to the harbour office. Now, in those days they were at the cobles; but before I was born there were just a few operating in the summertime, mostly old men and maybe a few laddies. Young men and the not so elderly men were in the herring boats; and the cobles lay on the beach.

When I went to sea first, I went in the coble, *Regina*; and she was still rigged for sail. I used to have to get the sail up. My uncle trained me in sail. I left the school in '26, so it must have been in the '20s. And the *Regina* carried the sail because the old men were very dubious about motors.

Pat Laidler and Jimmy Walker Look Back

From me being just a tot, I was with the boat – fishing. I was brought up with nothing else but fishermen. My cousins were fishermen. My toys were toy fishing boats. I was amongst the boats every chance I got. So fishing was in my blood.

PL

I'd gan back to the sea. I'd gan back tomorrow, if I had a life to start over. O, I liked the sea. I was never to seek for to gan to it either, mind. I was first among them.

JW

The Islands

The Farnes, a group of 28 islands, 15 visible at high water, lie a mile and a half to four and three quarter miles off Seahouses. An outcrop of the Whin Sill, notorious for their tides and currents, the Islands have been the site of countless wrecks. A beacon was lit on Inner Farne from the late 17th century, and a lighthouse was built there in 1809. Another, on Brownsman, was replaced by Longstone Lighthouse in 1826. Longstone's first keeper was William Darling, who, together with daughter Grace, took part in the famous rescue of the Forfarshire in 1838. The lighthouse has been automatic since 1990.

The Islands were given to the National Trust in 1925, and now attract 35,000 visitors annually. They are home to about 68,000 pairs of nesting seabirds and a large colony of grey seals.

Seahouses fisherman with cormorants' nests, Megstone, Farne Islands, early 1900s. 'Gulls' eggs', now protected, were once part of all fishing families' diet.

Now, Charlie Tinyen (Dawson) was brought up working at the Islands, which was a trade on its own. They fished round the Farne Islands. There's any amount of fishermen brought up off the shore here, but to fish round the Farnes was a specialised knowledge. As a young man he was brought up to it, and went in the sailing days. And what he didn't know about, especially, the Off Rocks – from the Pinnacles, Staple, Brownsman, off to the Knavestone – wasn't worth knowing.

In the sailing days, passengers were very few. It was just the nobility that went aboard a boat and onto the Islands. Anyway, I just forget which one it was, but there were four men aboard a boat. They were going away out towards the Islands. Amongst their provisions they had a little box of oranges: each man an orange. And this old fella, he ate the orange like an apple! Never had had an orange before! Ye see, ye're gaa'n back a long time there.

PL

Grace Darling

That's where Grace and her father entered the boat – a little bit gully called the Sunderland Hole. But it wasn't a howling gale as they talk about. Grace's father said that, of all the pictures that depict the event, only one had any resemblance to the actual scene. Well, there's no way a young girl and an old man could manage in the tremendous seas described.

AR

Beadnell

Beadnell, once known as 'Beadlin', was already a fishing village in the early 1400s, when tithes were paid by Beadnell fishermen to the monks of Bamburgh. Before the harbour and limekilns were built in 1798, lime, whinstone and salt were exported from the man-made haven at Bent Hall. Fishermen used this beach and the Haven below Fisher Square, where their tarred wooden huts still stand, to launch their cobles and load live shellfish into sloops bound for London.

Industrialist John Wood reorganised the herring fishing and curing business in the village, building new herring yards in 1826. Around this time, Trinity House identified Beadnell as 'the central place' for herring fishing on the coast. Beadnell's herring industry followed the pattern of almost all the villages, flourishing in the 1840s and 1890s, and dying out just before World War I.

Cobles at the Benty, Beadnell, circa 1920. The view looks north-west across Bent Hall farm stackyard and Harbour Road. The Benty is named after its bent grass. The coble on the bank top is probably BK 205 (R. Fawcus' Sarah Annie).

In the early 1900s, the Craster family were the main landowners in Beadnell. In 1947 Sir John Craster donated the harbour, the only one on the East Coast to face west, to the 25 Beadnell fishermen. When the south wall of the harbour collapsed in 1997, an appeal fund was launched, and this succeeded in persuading local and national government to pay for repairs, completed in 2001. Today there is only one Beadnell boat still fishing for crabs, lobsters and sea-trout, although boats from Craster and Boulmer now use the harbour.

My interviewees were: Jack Hall, who, though a Craster fisherman for most of his life, was born in Beadnell; Charlie Douglas, a Beadnell fisherman all his life; Maggie Fawcus, a fisherman's daughter (Maggie moved to Blyth when she married in 1938); and May Douglas. Although born in Bamburgh, May moved to Beadnell as a young woman, marrying Charlie's brother, fisherman Stephen Douglas. May has played a leading role in Beadnell for half a century, serving on the Parish Council, chairing the Women's Institute and acting as unofficial village archivist. I was also helped by Charlie's brother, Tom Douglas, and by Maisie Bell, born Catherine Dixon.

Charlie Douglas

My father left the school and started the sea when he was 10 year old. Then, when I was 14, he took bad, and was off sick for two year, and we had to gan on our own. I started in the old *Golden Gate*; then I went in the *Jane Douglas* for a bit; then, after the War, the *Sweet Promise*; and then the *Golden Gate* that we have now. I started the salmon fishing with Skee (Hall). He was a good teacher. 'What d' *ye* think we should dee?.'

Charlie Remembers

There's not the boats going to sea now. There was 16 cobles here at one time, when my father and them was young, four men in each boat, that's 64 men. Geordie Patterson's father used to say, there was 30 boats went to the herring fishing from here – herring boats, mules and cobles.

All the fishing was the same. At Newton, Craster, all over, there was a lot of fishermen. But now there's nowt doing. There's only one at Craster now – the other two fishes out of here. There's none at Newton. There used to be a lot of boats there. There's none now. That'll tell ye how the fishing's dying out.

CD

Skee Hall, his brother, Jack 'Fiddler', and Skee's son, Tom 'Skee', at the Benty, Beadnell, 1930. The coble is BK 75, the Golden Horn. Skee and Fiddler were related to at least six of my interviewees: Tom, Charlie and May Douglas, Jack Hall, Maggie Fawcus and Jimmy Walker.

Jack Hall

I was 10 when I left the school. The reason I left the school was, we had to go to sea. Well, I was supposed to go to a night-school, but I was never there.

So I first went to sea when I was 10 year old, and I went till I was 18 afore I saw any money. When they shared the money there was just my Uncle Skee and my father got money, that's all. But we didn't get any, the likes of us that was doing the work from when we was 10 year old. Ye was about 20 before ye got a penny. Ye certainly served your time for to gan to the sea.

It was all line-fishing them days. We used to gan away about 3, 4 o'clock in the morn, to the sea. Sometimes it was later. Ye couldn't gan till the tide suited. Always three men in a boat – sailing.

I went to sea a long time with my Uncle Skee. Him and his son and me went a lot of years. After 1921, ye know – after my father (Dick Hall) was lost – I went with my Uncle Skee then. O aye, a rare old fisherman was Skee.

May Douglas

I was born in Bamburgh, in the old Church Row. We moved across here in 1937. My old aunt was a bondager. She went to the hiring fair at Alnwick. The year ran from 13th May – ye were hired for the year. And Aunt Aggie was the best story-teller I've ever known, because she worked on the land all her life. She said they used to stand on the cobbles at Alnwick and the farmers used to look them up and down as if they were horses.

I knew Stephen before I went away. I was posted to Rugby making bombers in the War. But I think we got engaged before I went away. We came back home (to Beadnell) because, well, my husband's a fisherman. Fishing's in their blood.

May Remembers

The whole village is all altered. I mean, there was what they called 'the toon'. Now, that was the Church and the Church Row of cottages, Beadnell House, Beadnell Hall and Beadnell Towers, the post office and the Craster Arms. Now then, these (Longstone Crescent) weren't up before the War – there was nothing but a Square of houses just opposite. That was the old Fisher Square. They were built in about 1776. And they were pulled down when these were built. The fishermen came up here. Now, there was nothing more from there till ye got to the Stead, and they had to bring those up from the beach because they were

View north along Harbour Road, Beadnell, from the Benty. Cobles, left to right: Ocean's Gift (Dixon) and the Douglases. Old Windmill Steads can be seen on the bank in front of the present Steads (right), and the roof of the Square is visible in the distance (left).

getting washed out; and they built them up in front. Now they've got a house built on the beach again. Then there was the farm (the Benty), then there was nothing else. At the harbour there was just the herring yards.

MD

Maggie Fawcus

I was born at Dunstan Hill. Well, ye see, my dad was away at the War (World War I); and of course there was no maternity hospitals, so my mother went home to Dunstan Hill.

I was five year old when my mother died. And I had a step-mother – they were cousins, Mother and her. She came from London, to stop with us, and when she saw the plight my dad was in she wouldn't go back, and she kept house for us. She was a good step-mother.

My granny's name was Mary Ann Hall before she was married. She was the only sister of Uncle Jock (Fiddler), Uncle Skee and Uncle Dick. Skee was called that after a relative – he was Thomas Skee Hall. They called his son 'Young Skee' just because his father was called that – they did that with all the villages.

Maggie's grandfather, John 'Old Weir' Fawcus, Beadnell, 1927.

The Seahouses Lads Visit Beadnell

Oh, it used to be a great place, Beadlin! We used to gan there day in and day out. Weekends, we always used to gan to Beadlin. Well, it was very small. Ye had the Square, the Stead and the Benty, and the little village. There was nothing up in the little village. Up around the corner yonder, opposite the Church, old Dainty Dinah – that was the little shop. And the big house further along where Dainty Dinah was – he was German, Allhusen, in the Towers.

They all had by-names. Ra'phie Dixon and Teedle lived at the Stead. Then Bobby Douglas' father, Tommy Doodle – that was what he got. He lived at the Benty.

There was no other way to get to Beadlin but walk. Nothing else. All the teer we did was walking. We never bothered about cars. Aye, the bicycle … but ye were varnigh better off the bicycles

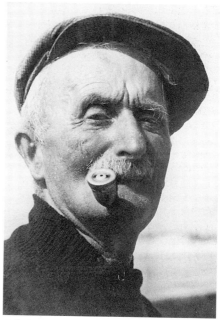

John 'Teedle' Dixon, Beadnell, circa 1930.

Tommy 'Doodle' Douglas with his son, Bobby, painting the name on BK 41, the Endeavour, at the Benty, Beadnell, 1933. The boxes are 'holly boxes', used to store lobsters alive in water.

than what ye were on them. And very likely rope tyres. Aye, and ye had to make the rope tyres yourself, out of old rope. O, I done that a few times! Spliced the rope together and put them on the wheel. Whae aye. Old boneshakers, as they used to call them.

JW

Mind, it was a regular thing on a Sunday night, to walk over from here to Beadlin, among the Beadlin men. In fact, pretty often in bad weather when the boats was ashore, we'd be among the Beadlin men – they all had huts. Have ye heard about the Square? Well, the huts were the north side of the Square. We used to walk over. And very often we'd be in Charlie's hut. And somebody might say: 'There's some sea on!' 'Sea! There's nae sea on. Ee've never seen sea!' Then they'd start. And I've seen one fighting against another, the Beadnell men. Ye'd just keep winding them up. But O, there was no animosity.

PL

The Black Huts

Yon hut on the banktop there is about the oldest. The Hayloft. It belonged Ra'ph Mitchell, the last man to leave the Square. That'un on the roadside *(with the blue door)* – that was the Reading Room. They used it one time for a fever hospital, O afore my time. It was always my old grandfather's hut. This'un *(the large hut facing the road)* come from Seahouses, last War. We come from the sea one time, and there was eight men in this hut; and Jim Lilley, he was the laddie – he was the youngest'un, and he was 80!

CD

Beadnell men at their hut: John Percy Douglas (centre) with sons, Tom (left) and Stephen (right), circa 1950.

Newton-by-the-Sea

At the beginning of the 13th century, at least three boats were engaged in full-time fishing from Newton. The village square, now owned by the National Trust, dates from the 18th century. As an antidote to sentimentality, it is worth remembering that this picturesque square once earned Newton the unflattering nickname, no doubt deserved by all the villages, of 'Stinky'.

Although Newton was a busy fishing haven in the 19th century, it lacked a harbour, so everyone, including the women, helped to launch the boats every morning from the beach. Several families, including the Beadnell Fawcuses and Seahouses Rutters, migrated to villages with harbours. Nevertheless, in 1904 there were still 20 fishing boats registered at Newton, some of them busy in summer at the herring. This had declined to 12 before World War II. Today, there are no full-time boats, and I was unable to find an older fisherman to interview in this village.

Low Newton. 3657

Low Newton, circa 1920. The Coastguard Watchhouse (right) was built around 1820 to combat a wave of smuggling after the Napoleonic Wars. It is now an automatic radio relay station.

Family Origins

The Rutters are really not Seahouses people. No, they belong Newton. Now, I can remember the ruins being there of the cottage, between the castle (Dunstanburgh) and Newton. There used to be a cottage on the links, and they called that Rutter's Neuk. I can remember the ruins of that place being there. Just ruins, mind, not the real cottage.

JH

We were Danes in the old days: Rutter was a very old Danish name. And the laddies used to say at the school: 'Ee lot were foreigners! Ye came ashore out of a ship!' There were two people founded Newton: The Rutters, followed by the Wrights.

AR

Low Newton. 6187

Members of the Wright family, Low Newton square, facing the Ship Inn. Tomlinson's Guide to Northumberland 1888 describes Low Newton thus: 'not pretty or pleasing, but exhibits itself to the sea as a village of pantiled cottages and stables along three sides of a square, where only the public house has a second storey.'

Lightning at Newton

Newton men worked the quarry all day and made pots at night. They only worked the quarry in the winter. Wrights at Newton – they worked at the quarry. They were paid two weeks at a time. And their pay was lying on the table in their house. And the lightning came down the chimney and their pay disappeared. Never saw it no more! And Rabbitty Dick's dog – it singed all the hair off one side of him. It wrecked the house, mind.

CD

Tom Wright (Snr) of Newton-by-the-Sea, with his lifeboat medal.

Craster

Craster, or 'Craucestre', the fort inhabited by crows, has been home to the Craster family since the Norman Conquest. In the mid-19th century, 33 herring boats and 17 line-fishing boats operated from the shelter of its rocky inlet. Twin markers were built on its two natural breakwaters, Little Carr and Muckle Carr, to serve as navigational aids. At the turn of the 20th century, 27 cobles and 10 keelboats operated out of Craster, and the village was home to four herring yards.

The harbour was begun in 1906 in memory of Captain John Charles Pulleine Craster, killed in the Tibetan expedition of 1904, and was completed 1911. Its primary use was for the export of whinstone from Craster's quarries, which closed in 1939.

Before the War, 25 Craster women were employed gutting herring. Today only two shellfish boats fish from Craster. One of these has a salmon licence. The one remaining smokehouse, L. Robson and Sons, established in 1906, now cures imported herring and Scottish salmon.

My interviewee from Craster was Bill Smailes, a fisherman all his life, who also contributed a fascinating written account of his 60 years at sea.

Herring boats unload their catch, Craster haven, circa 1900. The harbour was not begun until 1906.

Bill Smailes Remembers

I was from the north side of the village, and we all owned our houses at this side, and went to the Primitive Methodist Chapel, as it was then known. The school was C of E, and I often saw old Mrs Craster there from Craster Towers. They didn't have much time for us north side kids – at least, it appeared to me that way. You see, the whole of the south side as far as I can remember was owned by the Crasters, and it was 'Yes, Sir! No, Sir! Three bags full, Sir!' So we at this side were classed as the 'elite'. I don't know why, though; we still got our backsides smacked, and were lucky if we got one suit a year.

It's changed terribly since I started. I remember starting – I left school on the Friday night and I think I started straight away. I never fished with Dad because we argued all the time. I was in the *Silver Spray* with Dodie (Archbold). I've been at the fishing all my life, except for five year and seven month when we were minesweeping during the War; and I've been fishing ever since. And it's mainly been crab and lobster fishing, and before that it was a lot of line-fishing.

Another view of Craster before the harbour was built. The picture shows at least 16 cobles and five herring boats.

Craster looking west, circa 1900. Herring mule 617 BK, Elizabeth and Mary (Thomas Smailes), lies drawn up above the rows of herring barrels. The coble on the bank above it is Jim Stephenson's 194 BK, Unity.

North Side, Craster; the fishermen's favourite lookout. To the left is the gantry for the aerial flight from the quarry. Bill Smailes was born in the house with the porch (centre) and lived most of his life in the house next to it on the left.

Boulmer

Boulmer village follows the line of the shore. Its natural haven is sheltered by off-shore reefs. An earlier settlement, Easter Seaton, lay just to the south, and Sandyland to the north; the present village was established in the 16th and 17th centuries. Although all the villages had some history of smuggling, Boulmer became most notorious, especially for illegal imports of gin.

In the last 30 years of the 19th century, more than 60 fishing boats from Boulmer were registered at Berwick. At least 50 fishermen and three fish merchants lived in the village, although many fishermen worked in local quarries in the winter. Out of 32 households in Boulmer in 1895, 12 were Stephensons and eight Stantons. The major landlord, then as now, was the Duke of Northumberland.

During World War II the RAF established a presence at Boulmer, which still continues, while fishing, here as elsewhere, declines. In the early 1980s there were eight salmon licences and boats in the village. In 2003 there are three. My interviewee was George Stanton, a Boulmer fisherman all his life.

George Stanton Remembers

I started in my father's boat, the *Primrose*, a sailing coble, in 1929. We had an engine put in shortly afterwards. My grandfather's coble was the *Sunbeam*. Then there was a *Sea Flower*, and then my Uncle Geordie and them had the *Lily* – named after the family. I had the *Margaretta*, named after my mother, built at Amble in 1947. She was the next coble to be built after the *Joan Dixon*.

There were twelve boats when I started – mules and yawls. Mostly all Stantons and Stephensons. Them days ye had to wait till someone died to get into a boat. There were two boys for one man in a boat.

When they first got the engines in, they thought that they would frighten the salmon. They would motor to where they were going to fish, then use the oars. At the lines, they shot with the engine; but the engine was too fast while they were hauling, so they did that with the oars, too. Coming into the harbour in a westerly wind, ye'd pull nearly quarter of a mile. Two men on the oars and a stern oar. Long rudder on or no rudder on at all.

There were twelve cobles going from Boulmer when I started. But that must have been at the peak, mind. Because, before that, when my father started, in the wintertime when it got too rough the fishermen used to go away and work at the quarry. The fishermen used to walk from here to Craster, or to the quarry

Boulmer, circa 1920, before the road was made up. The building on the left was the Coastguard House. The coble is Bob Stephenson's BK 114.

at Little Mill, and walk back on a night.

But my grandfather and my father, they never earned a penny on the land. They were at the sea all the time. My Uncle Geordie used to say, if he got his crab pots in at the turn of the year, if he got two days a week he was getting the same as at the quarry – it was getting those two days in, ye know. They were just small boats, 17 foot.

Private Water

The Private Water, that's from Howick Burn, two mile north from here, right up to Hauxley. That is the Duke's Private Water. And he claims it was given to him by Mary Queen of Scots. And it's properly down, on this parchment, ye know. He claims a thousand yards from the low spring ebb. And we had a meeting, O years ago, about the worm-digging; and the Duke's agent, he had this old parchment out. And actually the agreement of this Private Water went right down to the Nanny – that's the north side of Newton. But the salmon fishing just goes down to Howick.

GS

Old Boulmer

Now, in the north bay, the North Haven, used to be what they called Sandyland. And that's where the village was. There was seven houses up there. I'm talking about before this fishing was on – the houses was up there, and there was a mill there, just at the brook-end. Now where the fishing is, there's a rock there in the sandy bay – and we call it Willy Robert. Now it's queer – was Willy Robert in charge of the mill, or was Willy Robert one of the fishermen? Willy Robert is connected with something in there. And there must have been a good head of water in there that time for to drive the mill – ye can see the ruins on the ground. It's lovely dressed stone.

GS

Stantons

In the Church records for the 1600s, I came across a reference to the Stantons of North Sunderland. They might have been crofter fishermen, because that's what most of the people would be: subsistence farmers and subsistence fishermen. And the Stantons were small landowners at North Sunderland. They moved from North Sunderland to Boulmer 300 years ago.

AR

Stephensons

There was a travelling preacher one time. He was going about from village to village on the horse. And he come to Boulmer. And all the teer he could find was an old woman gathering mussels on the rocks. So he shouts across to her, 'Hallo! Do ye know if there are Christians in this place?' 'No, hinny,' the woman says. 'We're all Stephensons here!'

TD

Members of the Stephenson family haymaking at Boulmer, 1920s. The horse belonged to Dick Hall.

Village Rivalries

Beadnell and Seahouses

Have ye ever noticed anything about villages? If ye look, all the villages on the coast, every one is separated by a burn. My mother used to sing a song:

Bonny lass, come ower the burn,
Dinna stand there and mourn.
Bonny lass, come ower the burn,
What the divvil ails ye?

That was a young lass courting a lad there, from another village, see, and she didn't want to leave her village to come into his village. O aye, in the old days there was a lot of rivalry between the villages. But they were married through and through.

There were little bits of songs we learnt. There's another one I learnt from my mother:

Eeh, what a life, what a weary, weary life!
Ye'd better be a maid all the days of your life!
When I was a maid, I wore my slippers thin,
But now, since I got married, they let the watter in!

I'm half Beadnell. My mother came from Beadnell; she was a Douglas. I've got quite a few cousins at Beadnell yet. Aye, there's always been a little bit of rivalry in the villages. Well, not so much nowadays as what there used to be.

TDw

We played football with Beadnell. Used to fight with them. And ye didn't have much of a football match – there'd be a fight. When we got out to Beadlin, it didn't matter who scored the first goal, if somebody was going to get beat, there'd be a sod fight. But there was no real malice.

We used to play the Townies – North Sunderland; we never played Bamburgh – Bamburgh was too snooty. Now, when we played North Sunderland, most of the team was hinds' sons. Now the hinds there wore big tackety boots that stuck out at the front, with a big toe-plate on. And, mind, when they kicked ye, ye knew about it! All the blokes my age, ye could run your finger up the front of their leg and feel the wabbles (lumps or waves), where they were kicked.

The Beadnell men one time used to throw stones at the Seahouses men if they crossed the burn. But that changed, because a lot of them married women from Beadlin. There's a lot of intermarriage between Beadlin and Seahouses. The fishermen used to fish together fine. And the Beadlin men in my time came over here, and ye'd meet them on the pier. Ye'd meet them at the sea. O, aye.

PL

Three Beadnell 'characters', Bob Fawcus, Jackie Douglas and John 'Teedle' Dixon, at the harbour, August 1927.

29

Boulmer and Craster – The Duke and the Squire

Was there competition between the villages when I was a young man? O, definitely. The Craster men used to come and pinch the limpets off Longhoughton Steel. And the Boulmer men said they were meant to pay, and sent them back without them. The Duke of Northumberland got in touch with Squire Craster. It got to such a pitch that the Duke made them pay! I think it was 6d a load. The villages didn't fight, exactly, but if they interfered with the fishing ground it got a bit awkward.

The Craster men were coming up the Smooth – that's easy bottom. They come in at Howick Howp. Ye went with them – dark, camouflaged. Ye put your light up, and ye start fishing. And the Craster men would be the south side of ye. So, the fish come with the tide, ye see. So that was a grand affair. Ye put the light up as they started there. If this man was shooting his lines, and another man shot ahead of him, this man would get in the way of that man shooting his lines, so he had to veer away. And as he had to veer away, the next man had to veer away. Aye, I've seen some fun when the fish was on!

It often happened, that. If that man was shooting his lines there, and this man comes and starts shooting ahead of him, and that boat kept shooting on his same course, the two lines got foul. What happened then? Words ye wouldn't like to put down!

GS

Squire Tom Craster, owner of Craster harbour, just before World War I.

Jimmy Walker with his brother Eddie in BK 72, the True Friendship, Seahouses, September 1934.

MORE THAN JUST A JOB

Crew carry herring ashore from 1073 BK, John Archbold's Maggie, at Craster, circa 1900. The smokehouses are in operation. The Rocket Apparatus was kept in the white house at the right of the picture.

The Fisherman's Year

Fishing is seasonal work, and all the villages followed a similar pattern. In the 19th century, the emphasis was on herring in the summer and long-lining for white fish in winter, with crab and lobster fishing in spring and part of autumn, and some salmon fishing with fixed nets in summer. In the 20th century, with the decline of herring fishing, the emphasis changed. Seahouses followed a rather different pattern, as herring fishing continued there, together with some small scale seine-netting.

As well as describing the pattern of a fisherman's year, this chapter touches briefly on other aspects of life in a fishing village: boats and gear, lost skills such as navigation by landmark, barking and tarring, village 'characters', women's lives, superstitions, weather-lore, and prices.

Of all the lost skills the old men remembered, navigation by landmark was most important to them. Each man carried in his head a map of the sea floor, passed down the generations and, so detailed, he knew it better than we know our own back yards. This was not just a geographical map, but a map of stories; references which, together with tales of village characters, bound the members of each community to one another and to the place.

In the olden days here, the main fishing was shell fishing from March till the end of July. Crabs only. Lobster fishing took place for two or three weeks between the seine-netting finishing and the line-fishing starting. Now, we went to the seine-netting on the first day of August. It was open for the month of March. Then it was closed. August, September, October, ye could seine-net. But after that it was closed for the end of the year. It was too soon to start the haddock lines. So that most boats would put a few lobster pots in, about 60, to fill time in till it was time to start the lines. Well, the lines continued from lobster fishing right on until the end of February.

PL

When I started it was seasonal work. Ye had your salmon and trout fishing from March to September. And when ye finished with that ye started with your

Ferrying herring from a keelboat moored out of shot, to waiting carts, Seahouses, 1920s. On the bank top was Braeside (now Crewe Street) with its herring yards. The Coastguard's house was on the end of the row in the centre of the picture.

lobster fishing, and that went from September until the end of October, November. There wasn't any closed season on the lobstering, but ye started with your haddock lines in November. Then when ye come to March ye had what ye call the 'night lines'.

GS

The normal time for line-fishing was from October till March, and then it was pots. In the early part of the year, it was crab fishing. No mechanical means of pulling them, so it was all done by hand.

When it came into the middle of summer, then it was lobster fishing. There used to be about a fortnight in June when they used to take the boats up and paint them. Middle of June, lobsters have actually gone to ground, 'holed' as we call it, and that's when they start to cast their shell. So there'd be a week or two when there was very little to catch.

So they would paint their boats. It would take about a fortnight. They'd get their engines overhauled and what-have-you, and also dry the pots. Got the pots up onto the shore and into the sunshine, and that killed off all the weed that was growing on them. Feathery sort of stuff grows on them if they're in the sea too long. We'd say there was 'muck' growing on them, or 'tath' – like a feathery moss, a browny colour. We used to get it on the lines, also.

When it came into about the middle of July, the lobsters were beginning to move out of the holes; they'd cast their shells and they were getting quite plentiful, and ye'd be catching them till October. Then when October came it was back to the line-fishing.

Bad weather stopped a lot of the fishing, especially in those days, when there were no mechanical pot-haulers. They had to be very cautious when they thought it was going to be bad weather; they had their pots to move out into deeper water. Also, the material they used for the pots then was not like the modern stuff – it was manilla. Modern stuff is courlene. It doesn't rot, which means it lasts longer, whereas in the olden days it was all manilla or sisal, and it chafed easily. It rubbed and cut through when there was heavy seas. Cut

Sailing cobles at Newton, circa 1910. The coble is the traditional boat used on the North East coast for all types of fishing. Easily launched from sandy beaches, it is thought to be of either Anglo-Saxon or Viking origin. There were 20 boats fishing from Newton around the time of this photo.

them along the top – therefore they had to be all mended. And after a certain time that stuff turned rotten.

The fishing's completely changed since I started. Mechanised things – self-haulers, pot-haulers, big engines, all the navigation gear which years ago they didn't have. Just had an old petrol-paraffin engine and a compass and that was it! Nowadays it's echometers, Deccas, radars – it's helped in a way to over-fish, because there's lots of days now they can go to sea, like when it's dense fog – in the past, ye just didn't go. Ye stayed at home.

Or ye might go, because it was a question of having to try and go, even if the weather wasn't as good as it might have been, to make a living. And if there was a storm – well it was just out of the question, ye cannot go in a storm. Nowadays the boats are bigger; they're bigger engines, they've got all the navigation gear in, so they can put up with a rougher day altogether than the type of boat they used here 40 years ago – different vessels altogether.

RW

The Coble

The coble is to me one of the nicest small fishing boats there is. Now, if you go and order a coble, you give them the length of the ram plank and they build it from that. The ram plank is the bottom centre one, that runs from just forrard of the engine, aft to the centre bottom of the stern. That plank is generally 22 to 24 ft in length. If it is 26 ft you will get a big, clumsy coble, impossible to work on with on a beach.

The next planks are copper-nailed and riveted to the first one. This is how: a hole is drilled and a copper two inch square nail is knocked through. One man holds a hammer on the head of the nail and another puts a small copper washer on the other end. He has a special punch with a hole up the centre that he knocks the rivet down with; then he cuts the excess end off with a pair of pinchers. After that, he rivets the end over: a lovely job that lasts forever.

Now when they start to go up the side, this is what determines if you have a good or bad boat. The good ones are if that first *landing* plank is laid with not too much lift, fairly flattish. Now, if he is in a hurry to get up the boat's side, and doesn't lay that landing plank as I've said, leave the boat where it is if you haven't already paid for it. If that plank is right, the boat builds itself after that. The planking is of larch and as a rule doesn't need steaming for bending. It is not a hard wood, but it is tough and lasts a long time if regularly cleaned and painted.

Building the Burn Crest, Northumberland's biggest coble, Dawsons' yard, Seahouses, 1960. Cobles are built by the eye, without a plan, using an oak frame and larch timbers. This one was 41 ft overall length.

Now, when all the planks are fixed and to the right height, they start to put the ribs in. Cobles used to be four planks up the side. Now they are narrower and have five. Better, I think, in looks as well. That happened when the White Fish Authority gave grants and loans for boats. The timbers have already been fixed at their right spacings on the bottom planks. So they just carry on up the boat's side from these. Generally, oak or elm is used up the side, and they are cut from crooked pieces of tree grown roughly to that shape naturally. They are much stronger than if they had been artificially shaped. These pieces take a lot of fitting, and it takes a craftsman to do it. I hope it won't be all lost. But the writing looks on the wall.

After this, the stern is fitted. Then the oak gunwales are steamed and fitted. Engine bed, thofts and floor-boards, rudder and tiller, and the chocks where the stern tube for the shafting goes through. Then the inspection box above the propeller, and the scut (the top of her stern). That's about it, except for the machinery. Probably set you back £30,000 to £40,000.

BS

Cobles at Newton, circa 1925. Engines have now replaced sails. BK 236 (far right) is Alexander Wright's Reliance.

The Price of a Herring Boat

They had a good year at the sea one year, Fiddler and them, and they bought the herring boat, the *Hepsibar*. £150 they paid for it; a brand new boat. That's what it cost them. Might be a lot of money, but they made that, a father and three sons all in the one house. He told me many a time. Aye.

CD

Launching

Sometimes the men sort of helped each other, ye know. Specially at the Benty Hole – they helped each other to launch. They launched both at the Benty and at the Haven. I didn't understand it, but it would be the tides or something. But at the Benty, if they were coming up for any length of time they had to fetch them right across the road. They had winches to help them; wire ropes. Ye had to watch yon things. The men got to either side of them and launched them up. Ye could hear them many times, putting their shoulders to the boat; one of them would be shouting – ye could hear them clearly – 'Howway OOP!'

MF

Left: Launching a herring boat beside Beadnell herring houses at the end of what is now Harbour Road, circa 1900.

Below: Hauling a boat up at Craster, circa 1900. This capstan was used until about 1956, when the Craster men finally got a petrol-powered winch.

Landmarks

When we went to sea, ye had to gan by the compass. Ye knew all the ground, because ye were told by the old men. For generations, it was handed down to ye. Ye knew all the ground where to fish and everything. Like the Middle Bank: Hebron, the Kill; and Staggart, the lighthouse on Sun'land Point. The Off Bank: Staggart, the Castle – that's what we called the Bratting Ground, what they call the Off Bank. They've changed the name. They'll tell ye, Aye, they've found some good ground! Well, they've fished thousands of years there! Ye just sit and listen to them.

Ye had to fish on the Banks at one time, ye know, where it was easy bottom. But now, with these different trawls, they go over hard ground and everything. So they're taking everything away. Anybody that gans to sea now, they divvin't need to be fishermen. As long as you're a bit scholar and read the gadgets. Old fishermen, we had to work with the brain. We knew where the ground was. But not now. They divvin't need the marks. They just gan with the gadgets. And that's what's spoilt the fishing.

CD

Ye see, in the North Sea, it's much like the land. Ye get valleys, hills, and places where it's quite level and smooth. Over the years ye get to know these places. In the old days we used to use what we called 'marks': Hebron Hill, or certain bunches of trees, and that sort of thing. The Kyloe Hills – three sharp peaks. We never called them Kyloe. We called them 'Staggarts'. And Bamburgh Castle was a favourite mark: 'Castle, the Point' and these sort of things.

Nowadays they just use the Decca. They came in about the 1960s. But then, ye cannot be absolutely sure that they're correct. The radar's quite good, mind. They use that all the time now. It's very handy indeed, the radar.

Of course, nowadays they've got echo-sounders, to tell them what sort of bottom. Whether it's sandy, whether it's smooth or rocky. 'Fest'ners' are rough bottom. There are quite a number of wrecks and all. See, ye get to know them by experience. Years and years. If ye get into a wreck, it means a lost net. That's a couple of thousand pound, now. And ye divvin't get any recompense for it.

TDw

The knowledge that me father give to me and that me grandfather handed down – ye'd have gone 20 minutes in the boat, two mile off – and ye'd say to me, what kind of bottom do we have here? And I could tell ye; whether it's pebbles, or whether it's sand, or whether it's hard rock, or whether it's pinnacles, I'll tell ye – and it's not because we have an echometer. It was found out with the line-fishing. And the knowledge that my father gave to me, of where all these different places were – it wasn't yards short of what the echometers mark. Marvellous.

But since the War, a man could come from the hills. And he could buy a boat through the White Fish Authority, and as long as he's got all these instruments, he's got as much knowledge as I've gained for generations.

GS

Ah, a terrible, terrible lot of old people, when they're starting to turn a bit funny, they cannot remember what happened yesterday, but they can remember 50 year ago. Why does that happen? Somebody must know the answer. There's important things will stick in your mind long enough – landmarks at sea – a fisherman will carry those to the very end of his days. He'll remember those, because he's used them so much. I went and got landmarks off my father when he was unable to go about. He had Parkinson's trouble. For years he couldn't walk about, just sat in a chair. But go and ask him the marks to shoot a length of pots on a certain place, and he could tell ye exactly the marks to

During the herring boom of the latter years of the 19th century, many coble fishermen bought larger herring 'keelboats' from Scotland. This one is said to be John A. Smailes' herring boat, Lizzie Buist Rennie BK 57, Craster, early 1900s.

use. What water there was there. And when to be there and when not to be there. But probably if ye'd asked him what had happened last week, he'd have to think very carefully.

RW

Barking and Tarring

The big sails, we used to bark them – tan them. Aye. They'd spread it out on the grass, get a hot tank going. Cutch – that's from African bark. Boil it in the hot boiling water and throw it over with buckets and ladles, and the brush, rubbing it into the seams. That preserved it. We used to do that with the ropes and the sails. Seen us frightened to go to the whist drives or the dances. Your hands is brown! Brown! Ye couldn't put your arm around a lass at a dance!

RH

You had an almost impossible job to try to keep manilla and sisal from rotting in the sea; especially the sisal. If you were among crabs, they would chew their way through sisal netting in a matter of weeks. If you hadn't tarred it they would be through them in three weeks. To counteract this, you used to cure the fibre as best you could. We used creosote oil, Cuprinol; but the best way, and the dirtiest, was to bark (tan) and then tar it. When I think of it – Ugh!

What you did was this: you got all your new rope and twine, made the rope into 50 fathom lengths with an eye in one end and a string mark through the lay every 10 fathoms; and on the last end a wall knot and crown. You would make up maybe 40 of those lengths. Your twine you made up into hanks out of the ball, because if you left the twine in the ball, the bark wouldn't penetrate to the centre.

Beadnell fishermen tarring lines at Seahouses, September 1932. Left to right: Tom Baxter Douglas, 'Old Baxter' his father, and Dick Hall.

Now, the next item on the agenda was to fill the bark pot with water; about 50-70 gallons of it. Our bark pot was one of the old steel tubs that ran on the overhead cable from the quarry to the bins on the pier end, loaded with crushed stone. We got it built on a fire, complete

Tarring lines in the 'yettlin'. Left to right: Tom Baxter Douglas with his father, 'Old Baxter', Dick Hall and Jackie Baxter Douglas.

with chimney. You waited for a fine sunny day, then lit the fire, put the 'cutch' (a solidified sap from the mangrove trees of Borneo) in amongst the water, and kept giving it a stir until it was all melted; probably two hours. The colour of this concoction was brown and looked for all the world like cocoa.

After a good while it was all melted and boiling. A man stood by with a bucket of cold water. Another would have a packet of washing soda. In would go the packet contents, and the man was ready with the cold water to pour in, otherwise it would all spill over.

Now we're ready. We have a draining tray up and back into the tub. This is made with a couple of sheets of corrugated iron. Now in goes the rope, a bundle or two at a time, poked around a bit and out to drain.

It took a lot of boiling, and our main fuel to do this was to cut up old tyres. They used to burn well; and, what with the smell of burning rubber and black smoke, it was just like Old Nick's hideaway! Yet folks from the town used to ask if we were making kippers!

When you got them all a lovely golden brown, you spread them out to dry. Into the hut at night and out the next day until they were properly dry. Then along to the Channelly Hole field to stretch them out and get all the turns out as well. They used to be full of twists and turns, which had to be all taken out; then back into coils again and the strops for the nets tied on.

The next job was to get all this rope tarred. You would have two 40 gallon drums of it ready. A nice warm day. Old sea boots on and an old dopper as well. You got the tar emptied into the same pot you had barked in but, mind, you were careful about the fire under it this time. One of the other boats left a man ashore one day to tar some rope. He left it, the tar boiled over, and the lot was burned and lost. We thought the village was on fire looking from the sea.

BS

They all chewed tobacco, the old men. Ye see, that kept the hunger off. Because they were pipe smokers. But ye can't get much out of a pipe aboard a boat, because there's water and spray flying. There was one chap – this day, he ran short. He had no more chews. Now, in those days, even after the War, before ye had the man-made fibres, ye put your new ropes through cutch, bark, to get the grease out; and ye tarred them. And this old fella, he cut an inch off the tarred rope, and chewed that. Hardy old boys!

PL

Craster from the north-west, circa 1900, before the harbour was built. Notice the upturned half boats, used as sheds. Towards the right of the picture, a bark pot smokes.

Some Old Characters

Shadle, Holy Island

There was one old fella redding the line outside his door. He was a very old fella, about 86; finished the sea but he was doing it for his son. His name was Markwell, but everybody here seemed to get a nickname, and his was Old Shadle. He had a brother, Gooseberry. And Old Shadle was the happiest man alive, 'cos he was singing while he did it, and every time he got a bit foul, he would say: 'Chuck it up aheight, it'll come down clear!'

And some visitors came along. There were very few visitors at that time; I'm talking about before the War, when I was a boy. A few used to come in the summer, better-off type of people. He had a great big white beard and a little cheesecutter cap on him. The visitor says to him: 'Ye live to a big age here?' He says: 'O aye. Big age, aye.' 'How old do ye live to here?' 'O,' he says, 'I'm just a young man. I've only half my time in,' he says. 'We buried one 160 last week!'

RW

Old Dode, Beadnell

Old Dode Hall – what a man he was! He was lying in bed one night; and his wife and another woman were having a bit crack. He jumped up and blew the candle out – there was no electric light. 'No, no,' he says, 'save money! Sit and talk in the dark!' Old Dode, lad!

CD

Dode Hall, Beadnell, September 1933. The old characters of the villages and their 'by-names' became almost legendary. The stories told about them built up into an elaborate web of cross-references which bound each community together.

Fiddler's Monkey, Beadnell

Old Fiddler, Jack Hall, he had a monkey: Jacko. On the Sunday afternoon ye'd often have a walk down to the beach. We were all sitting on the grass. And Jacko was there, with John Allan. And they had the dog. So all of a sudden, Jacko takes a jump. He's on the spaniel's back. And the spaniel away! Whae! Ye talk about horse-racing. Gaa'n ower them rigs in the big field – ee! ee! ee! – right to Alexandra House, Jacko's sitting on his back. By, Jacko!

CD

Me Uncle Jack and them, they had a monkey. Now his son, Hector, clever boy, he thought he would try the monkey with the whisky. And he filled the monkey drunk. Aye. And there was nobody got to bed that night. He stopped on top of the stairs, and he was just going back and forrard, mad as owt. They had to stop in the kitchen all night. They didn't get to bed.

Aye! And he blew the fireplace out! A lad, him! Whae aye! Me Uncle Jack had been in a bit late that morning. And he put a tin of Brasso on the range.

And he went away to get a cup of tea. And the monkey got a hold of that, and he hoyed it in the fire. And it blew up. It blew the window out! When my Uncle Jack came back, 'Mind,' he says, 'Ye've been a clever fella!' That's all he said to him.

JH

A monkey at Beadnell, circa 1935 – probably Jack 'Fiddler' Hall's.

Little Adam Archbold, Craster

Little Adam Archbold – he was harbourmaster at Craster. He was sawing some wood one day, sitting astride it; and he must've sawed the wrong end, because he tumbled off the pier and varnigh killed himself.

He had a little bus; called it the *Ocean Maid*. They were gaa'n to a football match and he went through a hedge. 'Shipwrecked on dry land! Never been shipwrecked on dry land afore!'

CD

Women's Work

People now, they divvin't work now. Old Tom Dent's wife at Newbiggin, she told me herself, she used to gan away the morning, eight and 10 stone of fish in the creel for to sell. Ah! She had them off, having a rest one time, on her own. A man come by. 'Will ye give us a lift on with the creel?' 'Whae,' he says, 'I was going to buy a new horse. No, no,' he says. 'I think I'll have ee! Ye're stronger than a horse!'

CD

O, hard life, the women. Big families, ye know, those days. No family planning. I can remember only one couple here hadn't any family. There were nine of us – seven children. I've seen my mother rocking the cradle and trying to bait the line, mussels jumping off the plate – trying to get the different pans on for the dinner. O, they worked hard.

RH

Superstitions

I'm not superstitious, but my father and them was – me uncles, the old men. If they met a woman going to the sea in a morning – O, bad omen! Especially a nurse. She'd be away to a confinement, likely. Ye might meet them in the street in the early hours of the morning, going away to the fishing. I remember one morning – I'll never forget it – we were going down past the Northumberland Arms, and just across the other side is the big house. This morning, we were going down past there, and this woman come out. It was the nurse. Aye. And my father went: 'Bad omen, that! I've a good mind to go back home again!' Well! What a day we had! Lost all wor lines. Aye. Got fast to the bottom. No fish, and a proper disaster. Bad weather. Everything went wrong. I was just about 15 or 16 but I'll never forget it.

And I'll tell ye another time. If they met a Priest or anything, that's bad luck. Well, along Fenkle Street – talking a long time ago now – my sisters had some visitors in, and one of them was a Presbyterian Minister. And we used to go off in the afternoons to haul the creels. Pulling the creels with your hand, ye know – twice a day. And we used to take people off, one or two, just for a trip. So, this gentleman asked my father, he would like to go out. He says, 'I know it's bad luck!' – he must have known. Ye know, that day everything went wrong, and we hardly got a damned lobster. And there was one lobster especially that day – I'll never forget it – it was striped just like a zebra. Lovely lines down it, down the side. Lines along its claws. There was one of the Professors at the Hancock Museum, he got it away to put it on show. And we only got a few. And all the men had got three boxes! A good shot, as the saying is. I'll not forget that! Aye, it makes ye think. Old people must've known something about that. It's handed down, ye know. There again, I had that experience myself, and I'm not superstitious.

Then there's the 'Articles' – them things! Aye! Ooh aye, and some kept them for food. The Article. Don't mention him. Or a rabbit either. My uncle – don't mention a rabbit in the house! My Uncle Charlie, by hell, if ye whistled in the boat, he'd give ye such a look! He says, 'If ye don't stop that ye'll get a dad on the lug!' There's a lot of superstitions that are right enough, ye know. Handed down for centuries. Oh, those things are all gone now. They don't believe it.

RH

One thing that is taboo is to use the word p-i-g. Ye don't say it. Spell it, call it what ye like, but don't say the word. It's unlucky. And old Tom Stephenson, before the jetty was there, he was coming up the sides of the rocks with a box of fish on his back. They had just landed with the white fish on the lines. And where those four or five houses are that were the old herring-houses on the beach – Mr Patterson kept these animals in there. And they got out one day. And they were plodging down through the Ouse, up to the belly in mud. He's coming up with a box of fish. And I was walking down past him, and he actually stopped – and I'll show ye exactly the movement this old man done. He had about seven stone of fish on his back, and he was a very little fella, and he stands like that, and he says to me: 'Ye see them there, son?' 'Cos I was only

Craster north side, circa 1900. Above Archbold's herring yard and vegetable gardens stand a number of halved boats used as sties for 'guffies'. In spite of widespread superstition about these animals, many fishermen kept them.

A bride 'leaps the Petting Stone' for good luck at a Holy Island wedding, circa 1925. The custom is of ancient origin: variations of it are found in several Northumbrian villages, including Beadnell and Craster.

a young lad, ye see, about 14 or 15 – 'See them there, son?' I says, 'Aye, Tom.' 'In my young day, they would've …' – and he put his hand into his pocket and got his knife out – 'cut their throat!' He hated the thought of them being there.

I don't know where that taboo came from. And the funny thing about it is that nearly all the fishermen kept them. They used to keep them in their back gardens and kill them off for the winter. They kept their own bacon.

RW

Ye always turn with the sun. Never turn anything against the sun. There were many, many superstitions, but that was the main one. I'm the same today. Turning the car, I like to turn it to the right.

Friday was a bad day. They would never start anything on a Friday. They would never launch a coble on a Friday. It would have to be on a Thursday or a Saturday. They would never change their job on a Friday. And they never decided anything on a Friday.

TDw

Weather Lore

They used to say:

Evening red, morning grey, Sure sign of a fine day.

And we used to say:

If the sun sets in a bank, Westerly winds ye will not want.

I don't know whether ye ever notice – I don't like to see the sun too bright in the morning. Never. Rather see a bit dullness in the morning. Then it gets out in the afternoon.

There was an old man here, if anybody asked him if it was going to rain, he used to say: 'Yes. It's going to rain.' And then if it was raining, they'd ask him if it was going to be fair and he'd say: 'Yes. It'll be fair.' Because it's always rain and it's always fair! That's right!

TDw

When the wind gets into the east on this coast at certain times of the year, it could last for a week or two, hanging to the east. And that would be what ye call an easterly 'piner'.

Sometimes ye get a ring around the moon: that a 'cock's eye'. And sometimes it's very close round the moon and other times it's away from it. It usually denotes a bit of poor weather. I'd nearly guarantee, if ye've seen a cock's eye tonight, ye'd have rain tomorrow. Same as if ye look from here and

Rowing out to unload herring at Craster, circa 1900. Among the keelboats at anchor are: 1073 BK (John Archbold's Maggie), BK 1056, BK 839 (Charles Archbold's Diligence) and BK 670. With only the weatherglass to guide them, the old men were dependent on 'signs and wonders'.

ye see the Farne Islands standing as if ye were looking at a mirage – standing out of the water, so they don't look as if they're connected – I would guarantee that rain's within 24 hours. And if ye hear the robin singing in the tree, it'll rain within 24 hours. You watch – the next robin ye hear singing, it'll rain. That's one of Father's old ones, that.

If ye see a new moon lying on its back, ye're going to have poor weather. If it's standing upright, that's its normal position, but if ye see it lying on its back, that's not good.

RW

All to Make a Living

AR: In the Fisheries Report, 1865, fish were sold by the score. It gave the prices per score, cod and codlings. Now, if ye take an average codling, it's a certain weight. If ye work out 20 codlings, ye could get an approximate weight. And by working that out I discovered that they were getting in 1865 the same as what we were getting between the Wars for cod and codling. But they hadn't the catching power. Lobsters were also comparatively cheap.

LS: They were sold to a merchant, Robertson. He had a horse and cart. Crossed to Beal, to the station. And they went away down south – I've no idea where. O, there was eight or nine cartloads used to go away then. There'd be about seven or eight boats, I think. There was the Kyles, Shells, Walkers, Cromartys, Lilburns, Wilsons, Douglases, Hendersons. There was plenty of crabs and that, but they couldn't get a price for them. Ye got – what was it? A shilling a stone for crab?

AR: And sometimes 10d. A penny apiece.

LS: And the lobsters was only about 9d a pound.

AR: Ye managed with the strictest economy. There was nothing wasted. Everything was recycled. Ye had to do it.

Beadnell carter Jack Dixon, 1927. Jack carried the crabs and fish to Chathill station every day. 'Uncle Jack used to be half asleep many a time, with two carts coming home from the station. One horse and cart used to be far in front of the other, but the other was still following.' MF

RhW: Then ye took in bed and breakfast in the summertime. Ye were never done. Never done. All to make a living. Because they got nothing for their stuff, ye know, their fish and crabs.

JW: Nothing at all! A shilling a stone! Tenpence, some days.

RhW: And sometimes 6d!

JW: Aye. Fourpence for the lobsters.

RhW: Wicked!

JW: Somebody got it though. But we didn't.

O no, we didn't make a fortune. Our pays were from 12 to 30 shillings per week. Not often 30 shillings. We used to get 4d to 6d a stone for crabs and 4d a pound for lobsters (old money, mind!). Those big codlings we used to get ripping, 10d to a shilling per stone. The haddocks might go to 1s 3d - 1s 6d per stone. Sand dabs you couldn't sell. I remember we landed just under half a ton of cod and sprags one day for £4 4s. Sprags were big codling, not quite cod size.

There has never been a lot of money made round here. We always got our share of shellfish and line fish, but we never had good places to go on the shore for salmon or trout, like Boulmer and Beadnell. Our shoreline is too rocky. And those red fish were what brought the money in.

We went to the worm lines for a while in the summer. We used to get quite a lot of fish. But ye couldn't get any money for them, ye know. The things were dirt-cheap. Ye did anything to try and make a shilling. If ye got a quid for your pay ye were well in. But of course, I'm going back to the '30s. A quid then would be worth a good lot of money now.

One year, 1930 or '31, Dad and his two mates had been haddock-line fishing all week. They had caught a lot of haddocks, and they must have been a fair price, because it was a Saturday evening settling night and they had grossed the princely sum of £17 and some odd shillings. Well, after the expenses, they got five shillings each. Dad gave his to Mamma and I'm sure she felt like a princess; very rich. I do know my Mamma often went without to give us something to eat.

Mending salmon nets at Boulmer, early 1900s. Although picturesque, village life could conceal real poverty. Men were prepared to risk prison shooting rabbits and ducks for the pot.

Much later on, there was one year we grossed £1,600, and that was a big year. We would get between £300 and £400 per man out of the £1,600. How times change; and for lots of things, not better.

BS

Poachers

Dad used to go shooting – rabbits, ducks, anything for the pot. He'd go up to the Fisher's Brig – Sir John Craster's field at the bottom of the bank; definitely out of bounds. Caught there, it would have been clink first stop for him.

He used to tell me what happened to the gamekeepers if they came upon them. He told me about one that happened on them whilst hunting. They put him in a big sack, tied the neck of the sack, put him on the edge of the cliff at Dunstanburgh Castle and told him: 'You know what will happen if you move!' Another night this gamekeeper came on them digging for a rabbit. They just got hold of him, pushed his head into a big rabbit hole that had been dug a few times, and knocked a fencing post into the ground between the crotch of his legs so that he couldn't get out. Desperate men, eh?

BS

Hard Times

My father and a lot of the locals were at their wits' end to know what to do to make a living from fishing. There were no fish, no crabs, no lobsters either. The year was 1913. He told me they were pulling their nets (pots) regularly and it wasn't worth the price of bait, what they were catching.

Dad and his mates had their nets in the sea when along comes this man who said he could give them work in Canada. So off a few of them went. I remember the ship he went over in was called *The Corsican*. They left their nets in the sea and told some of their friends that they could have what was in them for landing them. He told me, when they got to Canada they could not get enough money to live on. They ended up working for the Canadian Power Company where they were better paid.

Anyway, those nets that he left in the sea – I'm sure you know what I'm going to tell you; when the men went to bring them ashore, they were full of crabs. The sea is a funny place and, you never know, it may come right again.

BS

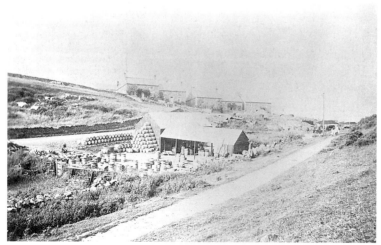

Archbold's herring yard, Craster, stacked with barrels, early 1900s. Although the scene looks prosperous, before World War I fishing was in decline and fishermen had to move away from the sea, to the mining villages of south Northumberland and beyond.

AT THE SEA

Seahouses harbour crowded with herring boats, early 1900s. Many of these boats, like the Morning Star (left), are Scottish. Right: steam rises from a boat's capstan.

Herring Fishing

All the villages featured in this book engaged in the herring industry. In the earlier part of the 19th century, men would fish from double-ended 'mules' of about 30 feet in length, often owned by the fish merchants. With the herring boom towards the end of the century, local fishing families themselves invested in larger keelboats of 40 to 50 feet.

The herring were caught in summer, at night, using fleets of drift nets. In the morning, the boats hurried back to shore, where mechants bid for the fish and teams of local women gutted them and packed them into barrels. The women became expert at the job; salt herring were shipped to Germany, Russia and the Baltic, and some villages also had smokehouses. Unmarried girls often travelled down the coast to Yarmouth, joining teams of Scottish fisherlasses who 'followed the fishings'.

The herring industry was declining in the smaller north Northumberland villages before World War I. Specialist Scottish and foreign fleets introduced more advanced methods, principally steam vessels, which required too much investment for the Northumberland fishermen, whose season only lasted from June till September. There were no local steam drifters. After 1918, drifters from Scottish ports visited Seahouses and Craster harbours, and a few Seahouses keelboats were converted from sail to motor. Between the Wars, many Seahouses fishermen reverted to mules, but now used a ring net rather than a drift net.

Herring fishing from Seahouses ended altogether in the 1970s.

The herring fleet sets off from Craster in the early evening, circa 1900.

Sailing Days

The herring boats with the sails – there used to be eight of them at Beadlin. I used to gan to the sea in them. There was one that my father had, they called her the *Hepsibar* – that's a Bible name. And there was a one, *Reliance* – belonged Dixon's. One they called the *Lady Elcho*, that belonged to the

Douglas. And one they called the *Chevy Chase*, that was another Douglas. And there was a one they called the *Eon*, that was another Bible name. I cannot remember the names of the other ones. It's too far back for me.

Seven men on a herring boat. O, they were alright. Ye had your living quarters, ye know. But when ye had big shots of herring ye didn't have them, because the herring used to break in through the door. It was just an ordinary door. O, I've seen the herring in there.

Ye used to buy your food then. We used to come into Craster with the herring. We used to sell a lot of herring in Craster, them days – and ye got a basket of sandwiches and a bottle of pop. Ye could get that for about 15d. Didn't pay any more. Ham sandwiches, beef sandwiches, anything like that.

We used to sell the herring on the boat. And the wagons came and took the herring away. They were sold on the boat, and ye didn't deliver until the wagons came. Ye sold them for nothing, I tell ye. Half a crown, three shilling a cran. That was 28 stone of herring for three shilling. O, ye got by. We were alright. We made a living of it. I'll tell ye what I got for my share for the summer – that was for 10 weeks: £7. Now that was a full share – £7.

JH

Aye, there was herring boats here (Beadnell). Not now. Ye didn't get much for the herring, mind. Different days! Some of the boats were 40, 50 foot. They carried a big weight, ye know. Our old grandfather one time put 112 cran out. So they must have been a bit size boats. It's about 28 stone for a cran. It's a good weight! Carry that on your back! O aye, sailing days. I can just remember them sailing. Just. I was one time in the sailing boat … Went away from the Haven to the harbour; but I wasn't up on the deck, darsay. I had to stop in the cabin! I was very little.

CD

One of the Grey family unloads herring at Archbold's yard, Craster, circa 1900. A quarter cran basket held seven stone of herring.

The Last Herring Boat

There is disagreement about the identity of the last herring boat to leave Holy Island..BK 152, the Brother's Pride, belonged to Robert Lilburn.

I can remember when the last herring boat left Holy Island during the First World War. She went down to Hartlepool. She belonged a Robert Lilburn – that's my father's relation. Lived in the cottage there. And I always remember – all the women and the people of the village went out to see it go; through the hemmel there, to the hill looking over the harbour – watching her going out, just a sail. Two big sails, rather, and a gale of north-west wind. She put up a record journey down, the speed she went, with the sails. She averaged 10 knots, I hear. It was the fastest speed a boat had ever run because of the half-gale from the Nor'west; following wind, flood tide – put a couple of knots on.

The *Thrive* – I don't know what it means, but that was the name; the *Thrive*. And I can always remember. I think it was 1916 when she went. I was six year old. Just a boy.

RH

The last herring boat that operated out of the Island, we know the number – BK 152 – but we haven't found the name. And I have a feeling that it belonged to a Lilburn. There used to be a hut out there – that used to be the fish merchant's, half way to the castle, and there were barrels all the way along. The boats would take barrels of herring away, salted herring, to the Continent.

RW

Women pack herring, while coopers from Archbold's yard fit tops onto barrels, Craster, early 1900s. Although it was almost unheard of for women to go to sea, women's work was essential to the fishing industry. Many 'fisherlasses' travelled down the coast to Yarmouth in the herring season.

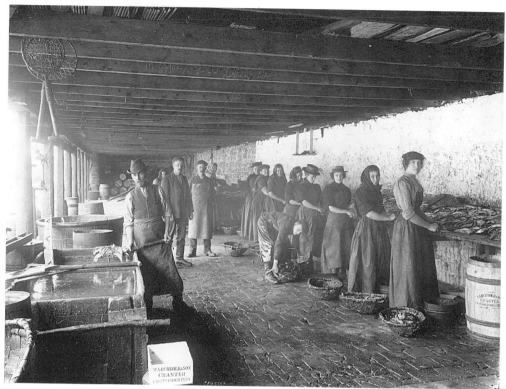

Women sort herring at the farlins in Archbold's yard, Craster, early 1900s. Far right is Meggie Grey. Second right is Lizzie Mary Archbold. The man bending is Big Adam Archbold. The words 'May 1902 120 barrels' are chalked on a beam.

Herring at Boulmer

Boulmer was a main herring port, one time. There were 40 boats working out and in here – there were two big herring sheds, nine men with horses and carts leading fish up to them. This was the best place for to take it to the railway. The boats would come in on the half tide, and they'd rest it on a stilt or prop. The weight of the boat on that when the tide went back would hold it. They had a paddle tug or a steam tug from Amble to tow them to the fishing ground when it was clock calm. This man, he had a sign – he used to put a flag out. And if there wasn't any wind he would come and tow them out. And the next morning he would bring them in. Yawls, they called them, the herring boats. My grandfather's was called *Thrive*.

When the steam started, that was the finish of herring at Boulmer. They needed fresh water for the boilers, coal and a jetty. So they moved to Seahouses.

GS

Finding the Herring

What they used to do when they were at the herring – they used to sail off, and they used to look for an oily spot to find the herring. Or they'd see the whales blowing. Or if they'd seen the birds flocking for the feed – they went all by them signs, see. That's before they had the echometers and whatnot.

GS

Craster women and coopers at the herring, early 1900s. Foreground: Lizzie Sanderson, whose brother James drowned in 1928.

Another way they used to find herring was by using piano wire. The boat was stopped and a heavy weight dropped over the side with the piano wire attached. When the wire was down to the required depth, about 10 or 12 fathoms, the man would just sit and hold the wire and feel if any fish hit the wire. I suppose he would know how dense the shoal was by the number of bumps on the wire.

BS

TD: Hey! Now, ask him about the herring squeaking. They do. Just like mice. I'm telling ye. The first time ever I was at the herring fishing, I heard them: 'Ee! Ee!'
CD: They'd gan by the birds – sollans and that. And they used to gan by the whales at one time and all.
TD: To find them, ye know. No echometers them days. But when ye first get them out of the net, ah, they're bonny! Far bonnier than what they are aboard the boat, ye know. They're straight out the sea, shining, lit up. Bonny little fish, they are. Aye, he's a bonny fish, is a herring.

Whales

There's not as many whales as there used to be. We used to see them regular. I remember Father used to tell me that, when they were pulling the herring drift nets up, a lot of the herring used to run down the net till it came to the lug of the net, where there was a thick rope sewn along the net. They would gather that up and they would pick that little bag of herrings into the boat – the ones that had rolled down the net. And he says that he's often seen a whale lying just below the boat with its mouth open and the herring going in! And he wasn't a man that would tell me lies, ye know. There was that many of them.

BS

They shot one night, my grandfather and them – they just got the nets shot out when a whale come up at the stern end. And the tons of herring were rolling off his back! And the nets went down. Full. So they started to haul straight away. Well, they got no much net, ye know; just rags and tatters. It was Friday night. 'O,' they said, 'the end of the week! Just keep hauling; we'll haul the rest of the nets and we'll be in quick.' Aye, the nets were all to pieces. But they got 50 cran.

CD

A record herring catch, Craster, early 1900s. A massive steam drifter and keelboats large and small throng the little harbour. Among them is St Ives lugger, Theophilus, SS 1.

Foreign Interference

I have a copy of the Fisheries Report of 1865. There was a Royal Commission went all round the fishing ports; and local men gave their depositions on the local trade. And it says about Tom Fawcus at Beadnell getting his head walloped with a piece of stick off a Frenchman! The Frenchman drove foul of their herring nets. And they had words. And the Frenchman up with a bit wood and he hit him across the head with it!

AR

Half-share Men

My grandfather on my mother's side (Richard Allen) was English – he came originally from Kent. He was a merchant seaman in the sailing ships; and he came up this way in a ship, and paid off at Leith. Now, him and a pal had the same ship – couldn't get a berth at Leith, so they decided to try their luck on the Tyne. And on their way south, there was a man got onto the train at Berwick who was looking for half-share men to man the herring boats.

Because a big herring boat took six or eight men, and there weren't enough men in the village for to fill them, so they used to take maybe a couple of Irishmen who had come over for tattie-lifting, or any casual labourer. And they were known as 'half-share men', because they only got half a share with having no nets or anything.

So anyway, this chappie, he drew a very optimistic picture of prospects at the herring: 'By, ye lads would be better off having a season at the herring – ye'll make more money than going deep water.' So my grandfather, being young and daft, and this other lad – they thought they'd have a fling. So they landed at Seahouses and got fixed up, and of course that's where my grandmother met him. So eventually his mate left, but my grandfather stayed on; and they got married, and he went deep water for a year or two until the family was underway. But although he had Seahouses words, he still had the Kentish tongue till he died.

AR

CD: Fellas with no gear nor nowt, they called them 'half-share men'. Sailing days, ye know. Some had enough crew. But if ye had to take on a half-share man – look oot! They didn't have a clue what they were doing. There was a half-share man – 'Organ', they called him.
TD: There was a party in Seahouses. He wanted to gan, but he had no clothes.
CD: They used to sleep on the boat, ye know. Whae, Jackie Douglas says to him, 'I have a pair of trousers I can give ye a loan of – they're ower-tight on me.' And old Hannah Hall gives him a great big pair of boots to put on. Whae – with Jackie's tight trousers, and Hannah's great big muckle boots – he ran along the sand to Seahouses. He was the first there!
TD: They reckon his toes were at Sunderland Point when he was at the Burn!

A half-share man from Shields, at Craster, circa 1900. With his seaboots under his arm, he would hire himself out for a whole season at the herring.

Three Methods of Herring Fishing

Hunter's tug tows out the Seahouses herring fleet on a calm evening before World War I. Dependent upon wind, sailing drifters were no match for steam.

Fishing Fleet, Seahouses. 5104

By around 1920, herring drifters were powered by motor. These keelboats heading out of Seahouses were probably from Eyemouth.

Steam drifters among the herring fleet, Seahouses, 1920s. While there were no local steam drifters, these Scottish boats were a common sight in summer.

Herring Fishing in the Speedwell

Charlie Dawson's Seahouses keelboat BK 174, the Speedwell, unloads herring, probably at Beadnell, before 1920. She was converted to engine and later had a wheelhouse built on her.

The Speedwell, now with wheelhouse, herring fishing, July 1926. Left to right: Tom Dawson, Bill Dawson, George Robson, Ralph Spears.

The Speedwell, herring fishing, August 1927. Left to right: Tom Dawson's brother Bill, Ralph Spears, George Robson (back turned) and Ginger Dawson.

The Transition from Sail to Motors in the Speedwell

Well, the herring fishing, it started about the end of May, beginning of June. That was drift net fishing. In the motor boat. That would be in about the 1920s. I used to gan to the herring fishing in the *Speedwell* – 54 foot long, twin engines, converted from sail. There was the engine-room, and three or four or maybe five bunks; and a cabin, if ye could call it a cabin. And them what hadn't a bunk slept on the sail in the fore-end of the boat, where the boiler was. There was seven crew.

Used to shoot their nets at night, pull them in in the morning. Went out at night, come back in the morning. Ye had to shift the boat down according to the tides. That's what ye did. Shoot your nets in the dark, then start to haul just at the break of day. Nets might be out, O, three hours ... Then ye pulled them in, because ye couldn't catch the herring in the daylight. They rose to the top of the water at night. Ye could see them swimming.

Ye'd go off for 10, 15, 20, 25 mile. By the compass. Ye watched the gannets, or the sollans as ye'd call them, just as the sun was going down. When the sun went down the sollans was finished for the night. Ye'd see them come down. They were diving for herring. Aye, that's what ye went by. Or the colour of the water. Oily, off the herring. Same as ye would put oil on troubled water, ye'd see the streaks. Ye'd see the streaks when there was wind. Aye. That was how ye went there.

I think there was nine herring yards here (Seahouses) when I was a boy.

JW

Women at the Herring

Now, my grandmother belonged the Isle of Skye. And they called her Miss Skee. That was her name. That was the reason my Uncle Skee was called Skee. My grandmother's first name was Annabel. She came over to Fraserburgh as a net-mender. And then she started to follow the fishings, the herring, from Fraserburgh right down to Yarmouth. And that's where old Tom Hall met her.

JH

Mother used to tell us – she travelled the fishings, ye know, before she married. And she used to say, when they went away to the summer fishings, they would never have seen a tomato afore. And one of them goes into the shop, and she says, 'I'll have one of your ha'penny red apples.' And it was a tomato!

MB

Fisherlasses at Dawson's herring yard, Seahouses, before World War I. R and CW Dawson had several herring yards in Seahouses. One (Ewing's old yard) was near the Black Swan pub. CW Dawson's yard was on the site of Swallow's shop, where these photos were probably taken.

Top two photos: Sorting herring into size at the farlins.

Bottom two: Packing salt herring into barrels.

Drift-netting with a Coble

The herring seemed to do something to everyone. It was just like a fever. They used to come from far and near to see the herrings. It was the highlight of our year, waiting and watching for the herring to come.

I've been to the herring in the coble, but we just used to use a short length of net, when they used to come close in. We used to go away at night with these five or six nets. And we had an echo-sounder, of course, which showed us where the shoals of herring were.

The most we got one night, it was about 1963, was 84 fishboxes or 21 crans in about an hour, and we lost half the nets. There must have been one every mash, I think. They were that thick, there would probably be hundreds of boats going about, and maybe about 90 boats would get nothing and 10 boats would be loaded. O Aye.

And they were that heavy, they used to just take the cotton nets out the rope, and all you were left with was the cork rope, the end rope and the sole rope! And the whole lint went away out of the net. And they did that this night with us. Ye could just see these great big squares of silver going away with the fish in, there was that many in.

Scottish steam drifter Adoration, BK 57, unloading herring, Craster pier, early 1930s. Steam drifters were able to use Seahouses and Craster harbours long after herring fishing had died out from the other villages.

Anyway, we put out 21 crans that night, the most we could carry in the coble. She was loaded to the gunwales. And I think we got £3 10s a cran. Today they would be worth £1,700. I'm sure if it had been possible to land all the herrings that were in our nets that night, we would have landed 240 boxes – today worth £5,000.

The nets we used from the coble were made of cotton and barked a dark, dark brown. If you wanted to catch large herrings you would use a net 27 or 28 meshes to the square yard. For smaller herrings, it was 30-32 to the square yard. The mesh size we used was big because the herrings we were after were always big here, and full of rows and melts ready for spawning. If they were spent (spawned) they were no use for

selling. I have been told that divers have seen herring spawn six foot deep on the sea bed in the Firth of Clyde.

Herring have spawned for ages off Dunstanburgh down to Beadnell, mostly in a depth from 15 to 25 fathoms, from the end of July till the middle of September. A shoal would be there one day and gone the next. You knew when you caught them how long they had to stay. Sometimes you caught them with the spawn running. You knew then that they would be gone in hours. Don't ask me where they went; but they generally fished them at Yarmouth after here in a filling condition – good for salting and making bloaters. Goodness knows what's happened to them all.

Many a night I've seen hundreds of lights where drift boats were berth for berth from the Longstone to the Coquet, seeking herring. They were mostly boats from Fraserburgh and Peterhead. Now you never see one. It was a most beautiful sight, seeing them go past on their way to Yarmouth and Lowestoft. They all had engines but they used to set their sails as well, and appeared to be racing each other. All were newly-painted, a truly wonderful sight.

BS

Ring-netting

The next fishing that came was ring net fishing. A big net between two boats. That started when the Second War finished. Ye dropped your light on the end of the net into the water, and your neighbour picked it up. And ye kept chucking the net out, and ye come around (in a ring). And ye pulled the bottoms up. And ye trapped the herring in the middle.

Why did they change to ring-netting? I think it was greediness. Well, it was all the hours of dark they could work the drift net. And when the daylight came, the herring went down, and ye could get them with the ring net. Maybe they would think about it before, but they would have a smaller net. See, when they got the engines in, they got a bigger net. Instead of being 60-score, they might have them 100-score. That's the way they worked on with the herring.

And the boats moved from here to Whitby and Scarborough, and up to Hull sometimes, up the Humber. Any amount came from Scotland, West Coast as well. Ooh, aye. They came down from the Black Isle, Fraserburgh. Seahouses harbour after the War – '46, '47, '48 – ye could walk from one side of the harbour to the other on boats. Nothing else but boats.

JW

Another visiting herring boat, this time a Dutchman, at Craster between the Wars. The crew are wearing clogs. The cylinder on the left side of the boat was used to haul the 'messenger' rope on the bottom of the herring nets.

Scottish motor herring boats in Seahouses Harbour, early 1930s. Seahouses mule, Ned and George Dawsons' the Blossom BK 40, lies just right of centre.

The Cluaran, Tom and George Dawsons' ring net skiff, Seahouses, circa 1950. Her name is Gaelic for Thistle. She was used for a variety of fishing, including ring-netting with George Dawson's

Speedwell. Left to right: Geordie Robson, George 'Ginger' Dawson (centre profile), Raymond 'Boosser' Shiel and Dick Nelson (with net, foreground).

They catch herring on the bottom now, with the echometers and the seine net. Ye see, at one time, olden days, ye had to wait till the herring came up at night time. But now they take spawn and everything away, through the day or anything; because they just mark them on the bottom. Well, that's the reason there's not many herring. Now the drift net – that was the fairest way for them. Ye just went by luck. Ye put your nets out and ye went by chance. The oldest fishing there was, the drift-netting.

CD

Long Lines

Winter long-lining was the traditional method of catching white fish on the Northumberland coast. In most families women baited the lines. Long-lining was less photographed than herring fishing, largely because it was winter work. This fishing method ended after World War II and was superceded by small scale seine-netting from boats concentrated at Seahouses.

Line-fishing with Mussels and Limpets for Bait

This was a fishing we were at during the period from about 1st September until the end of March or well into April. If you wanted haddocks you fished mainly in 25-35 fathoms of water. You got the cod and whitings closer inshore. But it did not always follow that pattern. Three men in the boat each had two lines of 700 hooks each line, making a total length of three miles of line. The boat would go slow ahead with a little mizzen aft whilst one man shot the lines. It took 30 minutes to shoot them.

You shot the lines across the tide, but there were times when you varied your course if you thought you were among fish, such as when you'd had a good catch the day before. You might turn the boat 180 degrees and try to get two ply of line through the shoal. I tried it many times, but the end result was not satisfactory.

When the lines were shot, you lay at the same end for half an hour, then pulled them back. If it was an easy haul, with no breaks of the main line, you were about three to four hours hauling; but hardly a day went past without a stoppage, especially if you were fishing on rocky bottom, which was best for codling. Some boats used to fish on soft bottom all the time to avoid the stoppages. We didn't do this, but I don't know if we were better off for it.

On the East Coast of the British Isles the ebb tide runs roughly north and the flood tide runs roughly south; so that if you have your lines shot east and west and are pulling your lines up going west with an ebb tide, you have to pull your lines on the starboard side (or right hand side, or north side). If there is a flood tide going, you must pull them up on the other side. If you don't, the heuk and snoods will be plaited up all the way round the main line, making them almost impossible to bait. That is the reason we always liked to use a mizzen when hauling, because the right side is often the lee side, and the mizzen kept her head to the wind.

We did not like to shoot our lines in the dark, as you often got your baited hooks covered in starfish when they got to the bottom. This applied mainly to the whiting fishery

Annie Jane Nelson (née Archbold) of Craster, baiting lines between the Wars.

close inshore. It did not affect the haddocks so much. I shot my lines in the dark one morning, close in for whitings. Another boat came out and put his over the top of ours. In the daylight when we pulled our lines up, his were foul of ours. Our hooks had nothing but starfish, his had a fish on every hook.

We stopped this mode of fishing in the early 1950s, as it was just not the way to treat a lady, with the work they had to do with bait and lines. For the men at sea it was a good job as fishing jobs go, but to the ladies ashore it could be hell on earth. Their hands were cut and hacked to pieces with the mussel shells and hooks. It was not as bad at Craster as in some of the villages, where the women had to go to the rocks and seek bait. We put the mussels into beds below the high water mark to keep them alive. In the first instance, they were bought by the ton from King's Lynn and Boston on the Wash and, being expensive, you couldn't waste them.

BS

Baiting the Lines

Your spouse got up the same time as you, and started to skeyn the mussels. She had to shell about three quarters of a hundredweight with a specially-made knife, and had to be careful to take them out of the shell whole; otherwise, if she cut them wrong, they would not stay on the hooks. The hook was put through the tongue first, then the gristle. Her hands would probably be cut in two or three places. My father told me he came ashore one day when he was first married and my mam was trying to break them open with a hammer, bless her!

Then the limpets were to shell out. Some used a teaspoon, others a mussel shell. In the meantime, the kids were got away to school – being careful not to put their foot in a pail of mussels or limpets or water or empty shells. Can you imagine the smell?

Next she had to make the dinner. By now the boat is ashore. Down to the harbour comes your lady; she helps you to pull the boat up. Then she carries one of your lines up to the house. (This was before we had huts.)

Then the job of baiting the lines began. This had to be done very carefully. Each hook had to be laid down on its side, with no point showing through the mussel. Sometimes two and three mussels went on each hook if they were small. It made the job twice as long. It took anything up to four hours to bait a line, depending on whether or not it had a lot of 'fools' in it.

BS

Three stalwart Craster fishermen, circa 1900. The three men would work approximately three miles of line and 4,200 hooks. Left is Bill Smailes' grandfather, Robert. The coble is either BK 41, Robert and John, or BK 63, Robert and William.

Craster, circa 1921. Although some of these cobles have engines, they are still carrying sails. At this time, line-fishing was their winter staple.

A Hard Life

Well, it was hard work. Very hard work. When I was at school I would get up at 5 o'clock in the morning to shell limpets. Every day of school, I used to shell the mussels in the morning. 'Course, at that time we had my father and two brothers at the sea, and every one had a line or two. Everybody was up about 5 o'clock in the morning to shell the bait.

TDw

JW: We finished the lines when the War ended, '44 or '45. The last one we baited, ye didn't shoot it. Na. Tossed it. Finished.
RhW: An awful life? You're telling me!
JW: You're telling me, hinny! It was alright for us, at the sea. O, the best job we had was the line-fishing, the men. Started about October. Carried on till March. Well, there was nothing to do, just pull the line in. Put the line out and pull it in again. Ye'd leave it in maybe about an hour. Ye see, it was the length of line ye had. The last time I was there, ye had 18-hundred heuks a day. Aye. And gather the bait and all.

RhW: He was a grand baiter, though! The mussels to do, you know. Off the beach. Sometimes limpets as well; but I didn't like limpets. They cut all your fingers while ye was taking them out with a spoon. A little teaspoon. Some used the mussel shell. But I couldn't. I just used the teaspoon. We used a knife for the mussels. We did them by the back. His mother taught me. There was only about four in the village did them that way. The others did them by the front. We took the shell right off, but they left it on, like a book.

Jack Hall baiting a long line – an unusual site by 1969.

JW: Aye, it was a rough life, that.

RhW: Especially when ye weren't born into it. I'm not from here, ye know. I'm from Birtley, County Durham; a pit village. Whae, we was engaged five years, so I saw plenty of it before. I knew what I was coming into.

We baited in the kitchen. Always. Slept in the kitchen and all! Ye'd have your swull on the kitchen table, all the water dripping out onto the floor. Ye'd have hessian pokes, like, to try to drak the water up, 'cos the water's running all the time, ye see. You're putting your hands in water and getting bait out. Well, it runs off your hands. And it runs out what we used to call the swull, that you baited the line in. I didn't like the basket swulls. We had wood. With the basket ones, the heuks gets inside.

There's two or three I've told, they'd never have married a fisherman if they'd had to do lines and the things we did. They wouldn't have the houses! We just had mats on the floor, them days, and oilcloth.

Craster, 1941. Cobles, left to right: Silver Spray, Our Brothers, Our Girls, Our Lads and (at sea) Thankful. Most families did not continue line-fishing long after the end of World War II. Annie Jane Nelson, seen baiting a line on page 62, ran the shop, second house from left, foreground.

Women's Work

When my husband came home from the War he went away fishing again. They were at the line-fishing. Well, I had to start and learn to bait a line, hadn't I? I had to learn to skeyn mussels, something that I had never done before. His sister had to show me.

On a morning, there would be big pails, and we would fetch them in, and of course it was winter-time, and we used to carry the pails in, and we used to have a roaring fire, because the fire never went out; it was the great big range, so you just used to rake the coals at night; ye put your pokers in the fire, and ye used to push them in among the mussels to thaw them. And then ye took each one, and ye took your knife, and ye opened your mussel, and scooped it out into a jar. Ye had your tray on your knee; and ye had all those to shell, and the limpets – ye did the limpets with a spoon – ready for them coming back in from the sea. And that's when the work started, when ye had to start and bait – 1,200 heuks. Sometimes more.

It all depended what time the boats came in, but many a time ye were on till 12 o'clock at night. Course, there again, ye hadn't any fancy carpets. Ye just had your oil-cloth. But everything was all scrubbed and that.

We weren't really at it that long – should I say a year or two, because those were the days when they were getting the bigger boats, and they finished with the lines. Ours has always just had cobles. But we finished with the lines.

MD

Hooks were attached to lines by cotton 'snoods'. In addition, Holy Islanders used lengths of horsehair. Right: Half a century after the end of line-fishing, Ralph Wilson examines a bundle of horsehair from his shed.

Snoods

JW: The snoods was mostly just ordinary cotton. But we once had horsehair, from Eyemouth. It was strong, ye know.
RhW: O, gosh, aye. Ye could cut your finger on it!
JW: And if ye got a heuk in, ye bit it out.
RhW: By, ye got some sore hands!
JW: Ye get the poison more off the line and that, ye know, 'cos the salt water's very, very dirty. They think it's clean. It's not. When ye've been fishing all day with lines, ye can see the dirt in between your fingers after ye haul the lines in.

Limpets

We used to go as far as Boulmer and pick lempets. We used to knock them off the rock as well, and they were used to mix through among the mussels when ye baited the lines. We used to walk, with the old-fashioned creel on our back! Ye know, the cane creel! And it would probably take ye about an hour or an hour and a half to walk there, and the same to walk back. And it would take ye probably about an hour for to knock these things off the rocks.

Not 'limpets'; we used to call them 'lempets'. Aye. They were often put on the heuk – if ye had a mussel that wasn't big enough, ye put a lempet on against the mussel and it kept the little mussel on the heuk. But they weren't as good as the mussel for bait. The mussel was the best bait. The lempet, he was a good bait for catching a haddock, but he wasn't very good for catching any other thing. The haddock used to eat him. But the codlings liked the mussel best. And they liked the mussels fresh.

But I remember, O I would be 10 or 11 year old, sometimes boats couldn't get to sea for ages and ages, and the lines would get smelly; and then it was the job of taking the dirty bait off and putting fresh on. But they would let it go as long as possible, in case they could put them in the sea and clean them. They would do that and generally never get anything. But I remember my father once going, O just out here to the Smooth; and they put their lines out, and their lines, they were black, rotten; and they got a load of fish off them. Aye. And we had never known that before. There's strange things happen.

BS

JW: Ye had to go to Budle, bad weather, five mile away, and gather the mussels.
RhW: When the mussels was finished down at the harbour, we used to send for them from Morecambe. Aye, they was nice mussels. Because there was no barnitickles on them. They was very rough on your hand, ye see. Some used to put a glove on for them. I couldn't use a glove. Then, if ye put your knife down there, the next time ye went in, ye would go down the same cut!
JW: O it was a rough job! Very rough!

RhW: They went for them to Waren. But they put them down in the mussel-holes down in the harbour.

JW: Put a bed down.

RhW: Aye, bed them, ye see. We had to go down on a frosty morning! Oooh!

JW: Ye had to walk five mile there and five mile back. The only thing was a cart. Go by the road yon side of Bamburgh.

RhW: Your mother used to walk.

JW: The Beadlin fellas used to come over and gan to Budle and all, occasionally, like.

Worm Lines

An unpleasant form of fishing that went out about 1936 was the use of summer worm lines. I left Dunstan school at the tender age of 14 years and three months on a Friday. I went straight into the harbour, armed with a bucket and garden grape. I dug in the sand until I filled that bucket with lugworm. Then up to the shed, where I baited a 700 hook line half a mile long with these worms. By 4.30 that same afternoon I was part of the crew of the *Annie and Nellie*. Three of us had the same length of line, making a one and a half mile stretch with a worm every 43 inches. Thank you, some job! I did that for six days for the princely sum of 10 shillings.

At sea, you put the float away, followed by 60 yards of rope attached to an anchor, which had the baited line tied to it as well. You put the boat on an easterly course going slow ahead. Then you dropped the anchor and started paying the line out until you had your one and a half miles of line on the sea bed (sandy bottom) in one straight line. These lines were left overnight, as we found they fished better in the dark. The fish they caught were mostly sand-dabs, plaice and whitings, but at times we would get a spur dog on every hook. They were like small sharks with a nasty spike on their back fin; and we used to get nowt for them.

BS

Preparing long lines – possibly summer 'worm' lines – by the bark pot at High Newton, early 1900s. Left to right: Tom Wright, Maggie Wright, Thomas Wright.

Heukkin'

One of the main ways we caught fish (cod and codlings) in the spring and summer was by heukkin'. It had lots of names: 'jiggin', 'rippin', but we used the word 'heukkin'. Each man had a set of these 'heukkers' with spares. The boat was stopped at the chosen place using landmarks. The right time of tide was a must: last of one tide, slack water, then the first of the next. It was not much use when the bend of the tide was going.

The contraption was made up of a line, generally tarred hemp, attached to a heukkin' rod with a lead weight in the middle. On each side of this heukkin' rod was a snood, a fathom of white cotton, with a ripper at each end. Each ripper was nine inches long and made of lead, which you kept shiny. Each had four hooks tied onto it with white cotton snoods.

The contraption was pulled up and down about a yard from the sea bed. The heukker flew around and the fish, thinking it was food (sand eels) got foul hooked. The water had to be clear for this job. It was a hard way to catch fish.

BS

Two Beadnell Cobles Heukkin', August 1938

Heukkin' replaced the worm lines for Craster and Boulmer men before World War II. It was already popular with the 'north-country' men of Seahouses and Beadnell. Above: Tom and Andrew Fawcus in the Sunbeam. This undecked coble was one of many requisitioned during World War II. Below, left to right: Bob Hall, Little Bob and Geordie in the Quest, BK 107.

Line-fishing came to an end as seine-netting became more popular. This form of fishing was taken up in Seahouses between the Wars. Only legal outside the three mile limit, it was only ever practised locally on a small scale; it should not be confused with industrial-scale purse-seine netting, practised from larger ports.

Local seine-netting died out in the 1960s when the Seahouses men found that they could catch fish just as well and less expensively with a trawl.

Seine-netting

The haddock lines finished because the seine-net boats started. That was a different fishing altogether. Ye were putting maybes six coil of rope out, in a circle. Then ye put your net away, then ye bring that other circle back to where ye started. And ye have a dan away, and ye pick that dan up. The seine-net boats have got bigger now than what they were then though, ye know.

That washed the haddock line out. We lost the easy bottom because the seine-net boats come in and took that, and we had to work on the hard ground. And if ye got a dirty day, maybes a day with the wind from the sou'west, and your boat was going away, ye catched the bottom easier, and ye broke your lines. At that particular time they went around about saying they were going to keep them outside the three mile limit. We'll not interfere with your fishing. But it didn't last long till we lost it. Well, actually, they did us a bit of good, because the lines was murder on the womenfolk. And we turned to the lobster fishing after that.

GS

Dawsons' Providence BK 142, Seahouses, mid 1930s. These double-enders were known as 'mules' and were popular for seine-netting, crabbing and even, after the sale of the bigger boats, for herring drift-netting, between the Wars.

Top, left to right: Charlie Dawson, Ralph Spears and George Dawson. Left: Seine-netting on the Providence, September 1935. The other mule could be Ned Dawson's Blossom or Robert Swan's Kindly Light.

Crabs and Lobsters

Fishing for crabs and lobsters using pots, known as 'creels' (Holy Island), 'creeves' (Seahouses, Beadnell and Boulmer) and 'nets' (Craster and Newton), has been a staple of all the villages for well over a century. In earlier times, shellfish were caught in 'trunks', large iron hoops with nets knitted across them.

Crabs are generally caught on soft ground and lobsters along the edges of rocky ground, often quite close to the shore. Pots are baited with white fish, 'shot' in fleets of up to 60, left to stand overnight, then hauled, rebaited and shot again the next day. Fishermen make their own pots, varying the design to try to increase the catch. Originally, there was little differentiation between crab and lobster pots; but, as lobsters escape more easily, pots with additional traps, or 'parlours', were developed in the 1950s to retain them for longer.

Over the last century, various restrictions have been enforced on shellfish catches, including a closed time and quotas for crabs, size restrictions on lobsters and a ban on landing female lobsters carrying eggs ('berried hens'). Of these regulations, only the size restriction on lobsters remains.

Beadnell, 1933: Dode Hall crabbing with his sons, George and Bob. 'In those days,' says May Douglas, 'crabbing was our harvest.'

Top: Hauling crab pots by hand. Left to right: Dode, George and Bob. There is a place for a hauler in the thoft; this would be removed for line-fishing and replaced in spring for the crabbing.

Bottom: Shooting crab pots. Left to right: George, Bob, Dode.

Crab Fishing out of Craster

This fishing has been the mainstay of the inshore fishing at Craster from long before my time. If you wanted anything new, like clothes or anything fancy, the saying was always, 'Wait until the crabs crawl.'

One form of fishing used here before my time was with a 'gerrod', or iron hoop, with a net fixed across. A piece of fish was attached to the middle of the net in the centre of the hoop. I understand that it was left for a very short while, then pulled quickly to the surface. They were hoping to catch shellfish. They used this in shallow water and, if the water was clear, watched until the crab or lobster crawled onto it. I used to play with these hoops nearly 70 years ago.

But well before my time, they started catching crabs here using nets (pots). My father used to tell me they would shoot a fleet of 60 crab nets on one length, about five to six miles out on the ground edge. That is where the real hard ground ends off Craster, and where you start to get the muddy sort of bottom. It is not a straight line from hard to soft; it is a crooked line that divides one from the other at approximately that distance. You can get patches of hard farther out, but I've not been on them. Men have torn trawls on these bits of hard, but I've not heard any results about the capture of shellfish.

He used to say, they would pull the six miles by oars and then lift all those nets by hand. They must have been very strong men. The crabs were very plentiful; they'd get as many as 20 stone out of the first 10 nets. The best-fished nets were always on the south end, so they would pull the first 10 nets on the north end into the boat, and fasten them on the south end. The next time they hauled they were still just in the 10 south nets. I have seen this happen myself, but have no explanation for it. Maybe the crabs are mainly moving in a northerly direction.

Let me tell you about crab fishing in my lifetime. When we finished working the lines, usually about the end of February, we would shoot our crab pots – eight strings of 45 nets. We would fish mainly four to five miles out and always the south side of Craster.

We still baited one line per man (three lines) for bait for the pots. Sometimes we would get a lot of codlings on them, but never any haddocks. They had all gone by the end of January after spawning. We generally shot the lines and let them lie whilst we hauled the creeves. We would use about ten stone for pot bait per day. At today's prices (1992) that would have been £600 per week.

After we shot our nets in March, we would not get many crabs until April or the beginning of May, and then they would start to move. I've seen us pull all our nets up and get only about two stone, then go the next day and get half to three quarters of a ton. I remember one Whit Monday we got just short of a ton. I think there was 150 stone. Most years we were quota'd to so many stones per man. There were that many, the factories and merchants just could not handle them. There was one day I baited a very small one-eyed net with a squid. The next morning there were 11 large crabs in it – perhaps the most I've seen in one net.

One of our favourite places was to have our nets north from east of Boulmer, just behind Craster Smooth. I remember we took four 50-fleets in the new *Anne B* and shot them down from there. The next morning we got 50-60 stone out of the dry nets. A lot of our twine was creosote-oiled and when you put them in the sea a great patch of oil would come from them. They were the best catchers of crabs – it must have been the smell. It's a wonder we were not jailed for trying to poison people!

Another great place to get crabs was round Boulmer Steel, about 100 yards from the shore. I've seen the nets full there in the months of June and July. You got a mixture of cock crabs and half size hens to start with, then come July they were all dirty big black hens and bad to sell. After that you went farther out and got all cocks. Then they started to cast their shells. That is when the male fertilises the female – when she is soft-shelled.

When the crabs change their shells we would sometimes get them in the process of casting. You would hardly believe that the new crab came out of so little a shell. Then they are the prey of everything that swims. We used to get nets full of them: you couldn't pack them in as tight – 15 to 50 in one net. You just opened the door and dropped them back into the sea. I think an awful lot got killed in the tipping out.

BS

Seahouses harbour, 1930s. Hundreds of crab pots lie stacked on the piers. Cobles were moored across the inner harbour. In stormy weather a boom would be used to close off the inner harbour entrance.

Closed Season for Crabs

All the boats went to the lines, winter time, except maybes two old men who'd work maybes 15 or 16 pots. That's all they'd put in. Well, look at the rest the crabs and lobsters got then. They weren't catched. Everybody was at the line-fishing. Now it's all year round, crabs and lobsters. Well, it's impossible to stand. Because they had a closed time from October to December. That's when the crabs is soft, white, when they cast their shell. Now then; they're in the pots, ye haul them; they're all dead, aren't they? It's only common sense. But the closed season was done away with. Brains of the country!

CD

Quotas

When I started ye put a hundred crab pots in. Then we increased it to 150. 150's the most ever I had. Out of 150, I've seen us get 160 stone of crabs. And the Beadnell men will tell ye the same story.

Well, that was alright when the barrow boys were on. What I mean by the barrow boys, the merchants used to buy the crabs – such as Robson at Craster and Dawson and Hanvey and them – and they used to sell them to Sheffield and Birmingham, to these people who were selling them at the markets, ye see. But then the factory came on and they got the monopoly on it. And they got as many as they wanted when the crabbing was thick, 60 or 70 stone, and then they put a quota on – so for all ye landed 160 stone, ye maybes only sent away 70 stone a day. When ye got your quota ye had to pack in, come ashore again. That was after we come back from the War.

GS

During the early years of my crabbing life, you just knew to within a week when things were going to happen. They followed a regular pattern, as sure as anything. All my time at sea, the spring has been the best time to catch crabs. You sometimes got a few in the back end but spring was always the main time. There have been times when the crabs have been so plentiful that it was impossible to sell them. You could hardly give them away – maybe ten stone per man, four times per week – and then the price was rock-bottom. You had a job to get a wage out of it. Today it is just the opposite: good prices but few crabs.

BS

Cutting up cods' heads for crab-pot bait in spring, Low Newton, late 1940s.

Over-running

When we were crab fishing in the '50s and '60s we seldom ever shifted our nets like today. What you did was to 'over-run' them. You heaved your first end up, then tightened the main rope up into the tide; then you hauled away, only keeping each net in the boat to bait and clear it out. Then over the side it went. (You had already put your end tow and buoy away.) Then the man in the middle had the next one ready for you to work on with. As a rule, about 15 minutes was the time taken to haul a 45-fleet so, you can imagine, we were not messing around.

Often, if you were hauling with an ebb tide and southerly wind, the boat would swing over the wrong side of the wind and you would be left hauling on a lee side. All the nets would be tight under the boat and you would have an awful job lifting them in. Also, the rope you were dropping back into the sea often caught the propeller – so a most pleasant day was had by all! However, we survived it all and I would do it all over again.

BS

Now, the Beadnell men, like the men here, never shot any more than a 60-fleet, which is as much as ye could handle. Say ye want to take them off, winter weather, miles from the shore, 60 pots plus tows in a coble – that's a lot of pots on the deck. And if she starts and rolls, and scoots them out, they gan overboard.

When ye're crabbing properly, often ye 'over-run'. Well, there's no time for to stop and say, 'By, it's a lovely morning, boys!' Ye take a deep breath when ye start and that's it! Ye can haul 60-fleets – we've done it – in 15 or 16 minutes. That's when the buoys is fizzing – going down.

PL

Low Newton, mid 1930s. A fleet of up to 60 pots could be carried in a small coble like this one.

A Nasty Gliff

My father had two men who went to the sea with him: Adam and Uncle Jim; and they called their boat *Our Girls*. Well, this day they pulled a 60-fleet into this little boat, and stowed them all on forrard. She must have been heavy. They wanted them shifted north, so they set the boat away and punched into this light northerly wind; but it was enough to splash water over forrard, which they could not see. Suddenly Uncle Jim shouted, 'The boat's full of water!' Father turned the boat immediately before the wind. He told me the water came rushing aft – he thought she had sprung a leak. They threw the nets over as fast as they could, and set to bailing with the two buckets. After a while, he said, they noticed they were getting the better of the water. I'm sure they must have offered up a prayer. Eventually they had the boat dry. I understand they came ashore after that, as they were shocked and pleased to get away with it.

BS

Barrels

The flour barrels we used to carry the crabs up the beach held 10 stone of crabs. We used to carry them full of crabs from the pier end up the harbour to the shed when the tide was out – often through seaweed up to your knees. It was not very pleasant. You used to be exhausted after that lot – carrying three loads like that on your back. You wouldn't see anyone doing that now; I doubt if many could do it. All for about 25 to 35 shillings per week. Wouldn't buy half a gallon of petrol now.

BS

Lobsters

Whilst you had all these nets off the shore you would work four fleets of 30 inshore. Sometimes we would get lobsters out of them. I remember one spring we would haul them and shift them about Billy Knock and a wee bit farther off, to the berths just inside the Easy Hole. Then we would go and haul our off nets. After that we would come and haul our four 30-fleets again. We would get between 40 and 60 lobsters the second haul as regular as the clock. Try and do that now and you won't

Percy Douglas carries a barrel of crabs from Beadnell Haven, circa 1930. This was the routine method of transport from the boat. Each barrel weighed 10 stone.

see life. We often went among the tangle close in and got good shots of lobsters – especially that place beside Cullernose, the Swinde Ends. When you got behind that sand that runs right up there and inside Billy Knock, you used to get both crabs and lobsters. I was shown all those marks up there by old man Archbold.

BS

I started lobster fishing in 1935, but the first recollection I have of lobster fishing was about 1932. I do know it was August, as the Scotch herring drifters were in the harbour. There was no money to be made fishing, and I know my dad was about past himself, wondering where the next shilling was coming from to feed his brood. Mamma was taking in visitors, which helped a bit. Anyway, Dad was discussing fishing with this old chappy from the Eyemouth boat, *Spes Bona*. He said, 'Ye know, Bob, the lads up our way fish the lobsters this time of year. They always get a lot.'

As I understand, Dad told Adam and Uncle Jim, and after a natter about it they decided to get 60 nets out of the shed. They were two-bowed with one eye – the 'Nelson' type. Anyway, they took them up round Cullernose and the Swinde Ends – dry nets. The next morning they hauled them and got a flour barrel full. That was a barrel that held ten stone of crabs. The weight would be around 60 lb for the night, and would gross them about £2 8s. They were happy, and I'm sure it must have been a godsend, because even then the stuff used to be scarce.

Can you imagine? I've caught lobsters for four old pence per pound, and crabs for the same price per stone. Anyway, the lobster nets used to be hauled two and sometimes three times per day. In fact, I've seen me go with one of my young mates and haul them every hour and get lobsters. If the water was clear and you kept very still, you would at times see them go into the nets. But I'm afraid that was a long time ago.

BS

Hauling pots by hand in a north-west breeze. Punch Dixon (right) with Geordie Fawcus and an uncomfortable visitor, Beadnell, September 1933.

Berried Hens

In the mid-19th century, lobsters became scarce and the Beadnell fishermen agreed to a rule against landing 'berried hens' (lobsters carrying eggs). Disagreement ensued with the Boulmer fishermen. It was not until the formation of the Northumberland Sea Fisheries Committee in 1890 that the rule was enforced and stocks recovered. In the later 20th century the bye-law against landing berried hens was withdrawn on scientific advice.

There was a restriction on berried hens. Ye couldn't land the berried hens, ye had to put them back. But that was just the bye-law, it wasn't national. The Northumberland Sea Fisheries enforced that.

After the haddock lines finished because of the seine-net boats, we carried the lobster fishing right through the winter. And we kept that rule about the berried hens for a great number of years. Then the scientists said there was more berries on a lobster than would keep all the men going on the North East coast; so there wasn't much point in putting the berries back. So then they started landing berried hen lobsters. Well, they never said they were wrong, but they found they were wrong; 'cos the stocks was dwindling away all the time. And they increased the size of the lobster. They used to measure the lobster from the barrel, ye know, to the tail. But now they measure it from the socket. They're over a pound weight, the lobsters they're putting back now, to keep the stocks going. They're putting a good lobster away now, mind. There's quite a few berried hens that's undersize to the new measurement, so that might help a bit.

GS

If ye have a hen sitting on eggs and ye take the eggs away, ye're gaa'n to get no chickens are ye? It's only common sense. But that's what they do. Ye're allowed to land the berried hen lobsters now. Take everything! Ye hardly ever see a one now. So that's how they're cleaning it up. This used to be one of the best places in the world for lobsters. Not now, mind.

CD

Gear

Making Pots

They make very tidy lobster pots and crab pots at Beadnell. O aye. We've only got three sticks generally in ours; but the crab pots at Beadnell are nearly all four sticks. What we call four-bowed nets.

We used to use nowt else but ash for the bows. Then we got the cane. We thought it was a lot easier buying a hundredweight of cane than seeking the sticks; and it was cheaper. Well, ye would probably spend a whole day, and the petrol in the car. We do occasionally still go and cut a certain amount of ash sticks in the plantation. We bend them, and they're all ready to put in for repairs. We got these around about Doxford.

This ash bow would crack now because the sap's dried out of it. We'd bend it on the bow-bender. Put the end in there. Straight on and straight off, and put a bit string around about the bottom to hold it. And it keeps it in shape, because the thick end tends to send the thin end away. So ye make it a bit longer than ye really need.

But ye see, there's no place now to stow your pots. They've got to be all left outside. And that's worse than them being in the sea. They're rotten before they're being worn.

We said to ourselves, well, there's only one other alternative: so we buy this plastic pipe. It bends easily. These pots are made with plastic bows. I dinna like them as much as the ones that I make with the cane. But it's come to such a pitch now, the cane is that expensive that ye can hardly buy it. We used to buy the stuff at 27 quid for a hundredweight; now it's £100 a hundredweight. The plastic bows don't keep their shape as nicely, though. They tend to scoot up in the middle, whereas the cane would stop nice and flat.

We used to knit all our nets. A cover would take me three quarters of an hour. But now we buy the stuff already knit, and ye just cut off the amount ye want. That's factory-knit net, and it's quite alright.

BS

Brothers Jim and Robert Smailes mending gear at Craster, early 1930s.

Bill Smailes (right), with Billy Patterson and Jack Hall, return from lobstering in BK 94 Anne B, Craster, late 1940s. 'Holly boxes' used to store live lobsters hang from the piers.

One-eyed Pots

To get back to the '30s: I used to do all my lobstering with Dodie Archbold, and always the south side of Craster, up off Howick and Howick Burn and thereabouts.

I recall one night we went away after tea to give our nets a second haul. We had this fleet up Howick Rocks from the Boiler right into the burn mouth. Well, it started to blow off the land from about west-south-west. It was soon a living gale. We were in no danger, but we could not get the boat's stern to the wind, so we just let the boat go broadside off before the wind, and threw the nets over as they came tight. We had no cover or hood up, only a canvas sheet over the engine box, and three or four tyres on top to stop it from blowing away. When the nets were over: 'Has anyone seen the tyres and cover?' No one had seen them go overboard, they had just blown away.

Next day was fine and we hauled our crab pots. We went to the *Children's Friend* for bait. We told him we had 40 stone of crabs but no lobsters. However, we did say we had three fleets of one-eyed nets to haul close in, so maybe we would get some there. I know we went to that fleet at Howick Rocks last. We had done not so bad out of the other two, getting between 50 and 60 lb out of the 60 nets. However, when we hauled this fleet that had been blown over the side, I had never in my life seen anything like it. There were two and three lobsters – and a lot of them were big ones – in every net. Where they had come from I do not know, as they had been scarce up to then. I do know that we ended up with 147 lb of lobsters that day, and most of them were in that fleet of one-eyed nets. They used to be a very popular type, before we started using trap nets.

BS

The Difference Between a Crab Pot and a Lobster Pot

We packed the line-fishing up, I'm certain it was in the early '50s. And we kept crab pots and lobster pots, mainly crab pots, in the sea. And then somebody came along and said, 'There's a different sort of net that's been made. Somebody at Seahouses has it. It has a trap inside it. And they reckon it's a good net for catching a lobster.'

Well, we used to have the ordinary two-foot lobster pots, with just one eye. And when we went on a Monday, we would see no lobsters, because they'd all been in, fed themselves, and they just came out! We used to pull them up two and three times a day in the summer when the lobsters were crawling.

Well, I had one of these new trap nets, and it was in a string of 40 of the ordinary nets, and I never saw it catch much. Never mind. I made 80 of them. And we put them in four strings of 20. And we couldn't believe it. Because they didn't fish anything – a little bit better than normal – when ye pulled them every day; but on the Monday when ye went back, there were twice as many in them.

Well, that was the start of a new era in lobster fishing at Craster, and we were able to cope with the money problem a lot better.

BS

Bill Smailes (left) and Eddie Walker in BK 96 Anne B Smailes, off Dunstanburgh Castle, circa 1960, with a 40-fleet of 'three-bowed nets'.

Billy Patterson (left) and Bill Smailes, crabbing at the Shads off Craster, 1950. The men are wearing 'baa'mskins' or oilskin aprons.

Salmon and Sea-trout

The villages in this book lie between two major salmon spawning rivers, the Coquet and the Tweed, so salmon has been a staple catch for countless generations of sea fishermen. There are two main methods of catching salmon and sea-trout on the Northumberland coast: beach fishing, with a T-net or 'heuk net', anchored to the shore; and drift-netting, or 'driving', using up to 600 metres of free-floating nets. In addition, until the 1980s, stake nets were used on Goswick Sands north of Holy Island.

Salmon is a controversial fish, also much sought after by private rod fishing interests in the rivers. For many years, and especially since the introduction of daytime drift-netting using monofilament nets, river anglers have lobbied to end netting at sea, arguing that sea fishing has contributed to a decline in salmon stocks. In 2000, the North East drift net fishery was reported to have caught 43,300 salmon and 39,300 sea-trout.

Sea fishermen are required to buy a licence costing nearly £1,000 per year if they want to fish for salmon. In 1991 there were 121 licences on the Northumberland coast. As no new licences are issued, by 2002 the number had dropped to 68. The latest proposals include a £2 million compensation package from private fishing interests to buy out the remaining sea licences. At the time of writing, the deal has been accepted by all but a handful of fishermen.

Licences

They fished salmon here for generations without a licence. Now, ye've got to have a licence – £850 (1992). And we haven't got a river! Same thing with drift-netting. Salmon – that's the big man's sport again. It's going to be stopped altogether, the salmon. If you're a big man in the river with a rod you're alright. But the poor man out there, he's not allowed to make a living now.

CD

There's hardly any salmon this year, for all that their licence is over £800. They didn't used to pay a licence, their fathers and grandfathers. Between Tyne and Tweed – this was no man's land. It wasn't until 1952 or '53 that the licence came in. Uncle Bill (Douglas) that was the Fishery Officer, he fought with the River Authority over this. Because they had never paid a licence. And it's just gone up and up and up.

MD

Bill Dixon with salmon, Beadnell harbour, circa 1930. The biggest salmon ever landed at Beadnell, caught by Old Weir Fawcus in the beach nets where the yachts are now moored, is said to have weighed 64 lb.

Stake Nets

TD: There used to be stake nets here, like they have at Goswick – ooh, afore my time. But I've heard them talk about it. I've seen the ends of the stakes cocking up out of the sand.

CD: Seen them along at the Burn. Aye.

Salmon stake nets. The salmon were stranded as the tide ebbed. This kind of fishing, once commonplace on the Northumberland coast, was banned south of Holy Island by the Tweed Act of 1854; but it continued on Goswick Sands north of Holy Island until the 1980s. Above: Stake nets at Holy Island, circa 1900. Women and children appear to be helping. Below: Goswick Sands, circa 1905. In 1960 over 900 salmon were caught in one day in these nets.

Beach Nets

The main trouting berths here were: Sand End – that's half way between Renner's Nick and the Burn; Robin Wood's Rock – that's a low water berth. Featherblaa' – well, we fish that yet. Back of the Carrs – that's low water again. The Cundy. Then there's the Pier Stones; Kill Corner when there's big tides. And the Point.

We work a heuk net on the beach. We put it together ourselves. The heuk and the running net. The bag is nylon, the rest is monofilament. Ye add a net on or take a net off as the tide comes in or gans back. With the old nets, salmon would get trapped in the heuk, in the bag. But now, with these monofilament – whae, they get catched in the mashes, anywhere along. It used to be a six inch mash in the hemp net. We lost hundreds of fish that way. Now it's a four inch mash for the running net, four and a quarter for the heuk. A driving net's a five inch mash.

Boulmer and Amble work a different net to us. Theirs has a flood tide trap and an ebb tide trap. Whae, there's 10 hours' ebb tide in this bay. There's hardly any flood tide at all; it eddies round the bay, and it's all ebb. So we only work the ebb tide heuk. The nets they have at Boulmer – they have what they call a 'monk' – a funnel into the bag. The hole into the trap is very small on our net.

CD

Hauling beach nets at the Cundy, Beadnell Bay, August 1933. George (left) and Bob Hall, with their father Dode on oars. Although salmon are also caught, beach net fishing at Beadnell is mostly for sea-trout.

There wasn't any drift-netting when I was young. When I started, we were just on the beach with the T-net. There's different berths for the salmon, but that's just a gentlemen's agreement, that. What they do is spend one day on the south half and one day on the north half. So everybody gets a fair chance.

All the berths have names. There's Seaton Point, Bally Carr, the Haven, Sammy's Bank, Thue's House, the Carr Road, the Little Sett and the Far Sett, the Bally Stones – Ballast stones – then ye're getting down to Amble there. The north side – that's an interesting one. Ye've got Howick Burn, Island Skeers, the Black Stone, and the North Haven, we call it. That used to be a great place for trout. Before they made agreement for the berths, they used to go away on a Sunday night to keep that berth, lying there all night to get the berth for the next day.

GS

Manilla nets took a great deal of maintenance. Here, the Halls mend salmon nets behind Harbour Road, Beadnell, August 1927. Left: Dode Hall, on the right, with sons Bob and George, and Tommy Douglas. Right: Bob and Dode, with the Benty cottages in the background.

Night Fishing

We first of all used to go night fishing up off the Coquet, leaving Craster about 7 pm and getting back about 7 am. There used to be tons of jellyfish in the nets and all the rubbish imaginable – thousands of plastic bags, old gates, naily fence posts – and I remember after a heavy rain storm with flooding, somebody's wooden bungalow! Anyway, this night lark lasted quite a few years, until we found we could catch them during daylight. That made the job much easier.

BS

How to Catch a Salmon

I'll tell you, when you think you've got the answer on how to catch a salmon drift-netting, forget it, and start from scratch the next day. Salmon fishing was one of the most exasperating jobs you ever went to. As sure as death, you would be in the right place at the wrong time, or your nets would bunch up when you wanted them to stay straight, or go north and south when you wanted them to stay east and west. Generally, you get the salmon when the tide is easing and the start of the next tide. You get a few while the full bend of the tide is going, but all salmon fishermen look to getting the best out of their nets across the slack water.

I got my salmon licence in 1963. We just used nylon nets then. We used to get quite a lot of fish in them; but at the finish we could not get any fish in them at all during the day. Yet in the '60s and '70s we got plenty of fish in them during the day. Some years blue nets would catch them; then, when you bought blue nets for the next year, the man who had all the green nets was best boat. Bill Dixon used a lot of white nets and he fished well with them. A lot used to depend on the colour of the sky, colour of the water. If it's breezy it's OK – not too much wind, though. Calm water is no use generally; but I've seen 17 salmon hit the net in one heap on a calm day. You just can't figure them out.

If you think you've got the correct answer on what to do to catch a salmon, forget it. You haven't. They will prove you know nowt the next day.

BS

Tides

We used to like fishing for the salmon down off Holy Island, as you were seldom troubled by seals. I understand it is a different story now. It wasn't a big area where you could fish legally. If you went too far north you got onto the Berwick side and you had to be very careful. The tides were always very contrary down there, and you had to be careful where you went at what stage of the tide. It was most dangerous beside that North Goldstone rock. It used to go overhead when the tide was up. The tides always seemed to be contrary there as well. Some days, when we put our nets out close to the rock after looking at the tide book and thinking we would go away from it, the opposite happened, and it was all hands to action stations.

BS

Seals

When I started with a salmon licence in the early '60s, you were reasonably certain to get most of the fish that went into your nets. Of course, it wasn't long before 'You Know Who' came on the scene. They used to lie in wait outside the harbour and as soon as you started your engine up it was like the gathering of the clans. They followed you all the way until you put your nets in the water. Then they paraded back and forth along your nets. If you fired the rifle he would just not take one blind bit of notice of the bullet smacking into the water beside him. Nine times out of ten he would dive but just come up somewhere else. I'm sure they thought we were playing a game with them.

Generally, if you went three to six miles out you were clear of them, but it was not very often that you got salmon that far out. I think that the 26 years I fished for salmon you could count on one hand the times I got any quantity of fish out there, and I mean between 20 and 40. The most are caught between 50 yards and two and a half miles from the shore. The best level is between one and two miles. That is where we mainly fished, regardless.

We were always looking at the nets in case a fish hit them. You would see the splash and go and take it out if you got there first. At least, that was the idea. You went full-speed to see if you were going to be lucky. Not likely! I've seen them tear out 21 salmon before 7 am. All that was there was a mass of silver scales and a hole you could drive a car through. They can destroy a half net in a couple of days, and that is £70 or £80.

You hear folks on about them being nice, cuddly animals. Don't you believe it. I'm sure there are too many of them. It is getting worse every year. The salmon are getting more scarce and the animals are getting more numerous. So what happens to the inshore fisherman in the middle?

BS

R. Carrs of Newton's three-planked coble, Mabel 281 BK, at the salmon nets near the berth known as 'Jenny', in the shadow of Dunstanburgh Castle, before World War I.

Not, as the caption claims, a brat (turbot) net, which had a wide mesh, but a salmon net, prepared at Low Newton, circa 1910.

A Record Catch

I used to be always very particular with my salmon nets. They were always clean, never any holes in them, always properly mended, etc. Now, there was another fellow just the opposite. He never bothered with his nets and his boat used to smell to high heavens. I'll tell you, though, you couldn't foot (beat) him for catching a salmon. I remember coming ashore one night:

'Got any fish, Bill?'

'Yes, love. We've done well today. We've had 112.'

I sat down to my dinner, 8 or 9 pm. Edith said, 'I'll just have a look and see who else is ashore.'

I was sitting enjoying my meal when I was pulled back to life from dreaming by a voice from the room:

'Bill, there's a boat at the beach and I think there's something the matter with it. The stern is right down in the water and the boat's head is right up in the air.'

I went and had a look, and what I saw put me off my dinner. The boat was loaded with big salmon – 250 of them, a record I don't think has been passed by anyone in one day. His nets had gone all shapes and had stopped amongst the salmon all day. He told me that the seals were taking them out as fast as he was. It must have been some shoal.

His boat and nets were the scruffiest you ever saw, but for three or four years he used to almost double everybody every day.

BS

Where to Shoot Your Nets

When you put your salmon nets in the sea, you always made sure you were at least no nearer than half to three quarters of a mile either side of your neighbour. I mean north side or south side. It didn't matter how close you were the east or west side, as long as your nets drifted clear of each other. Most boats always liked to get on the south side of all the other boats, providing that was the level you thought the fish were. Some of the Boulmer boats were good hands at putting their nets in the water close the south side of you. They never put them in the sea close the north side of you. You see, fish (salmon) generally are swimming north and most that you get are meshed from the south side. You get an odd one from the north side, but not many.

I recall one Saturday morning off Craster, we had our nets in the sea and were getting quite a few salmon. We must have been the only lucky one that day because there were four boats came and shot around us, north, south, east and west. We were little p***y in the middle and they were no more than 200 or 300 yards from us. None of them had any fish. We ended up at 12 noon with 42. That is what happened; and shall I add that it contradicts a lot of what I've told you about what we think happens. They are the most unpredictable fish that swim in the sea; so don't make plans on how to catch them.

BS

Drying unbarked salmon nets at Boulmer, circa 1920. Before man-made fibres and monofilament, nets had to be dried every weekend.

Poaching Before the War

After the season finished, in the back end, they all went poaching salmon before the War. Everybody did it. Survival, I suppose. Dad used to tell me about an uncle of his; I don't know anything about him, except that he was an old tyrant, who used to wear a great big 'wideawake' hat – whatever that was! He was before my time, thank goodness. Every time he was within range of any of the youngsters, he used to take this hat off and give them a switch around the lug. 'Take that! Ye know what that's for!' His by-name was 'Dice'.

Anyway, he was on this poaching lark. They were hauling the net, and couldn't get the last net-end as a water-bailiff was hanging on to the end. The old boy jumps over the boat's stern with the short tiller in his hand. He gives the bailey the works, jumps back into the boat, and off. I was told he had to remain hidden for three weeks amongst the herring nets in the loft till the heat died down.

BS

Afore my time, I've heard them say, when the salmon poaching was on, they used to hoy one into the pub door. Then they went and hoyed another into the Coastguard's door. Then they hoyed a one into the Policeman's. 'Now,' they'd say: 'Ye'd better say nothing. Ye've had your share!' They'd sell the rest. O, aye – ye'd get as many salmon as ye liked for 6d a pound. They all had their share, afore they started to make the money, olden days, afore the First World War.

JH

FOR THOSE IN PERIL

Unknown shipwreck at Craster, circa 1900.

The sea is a dangerous place, and the Northumberland coast has seen a great deal of unrecorded tragedy and heroism. The first dedicated lifeboat in the British Isles was stationed at Bamburgh in the late 1700s and crewed by Seahouses fishermen. The 19th century saw lifeboats stationed at Holy Island, North Sunderland and Boulmer. Other villages, including Beadnell and Craster, maintained 'Volunteer Lifesaving Societies', with rocket equipment transported by horse and cart.

Many of the fishermen I interviewed, including Robin Henderson, George Livingston Shell, Jimmy Walker and George Stanton, served on the lifeboats; Ralph Wilson of Holy Island and Tom Dawson of Seahouses were Coxswains. All had, in addition, lived through one or both World Wars. The following is a small selection from their memories.

Sailing Days Shipwreck

Now, the old men one time told me, there was an awful storm from the south-east. And there was a ship coming, and he lost his sails in the gale. And he just come afore the wind. And the old men says, 'Now, he'll gan ashore Sun'land Point.' And they went off along the sand. And afore they got there, I've heard them say, there was one sea hit him. Oh! By the time they got to the Point, there was nothing but matchwood! Nothing but matchwood, aye. All drowned. She had lost her sails, ye see, and he just had to come afore the wind.

CD

Barkentine HJ Jensen ashore at the Cusha, Craster. The card is postmarked 1909.

The October Gale, 14th October 1881

It was a fine morning. Old Selby Allison and Alfred Chapman – they went down to the harbour where the punt-house was. Calm day, water smooth as a glass. I've heard my grandfather tell me about it. That was the day when the October Gale was, and there were 129 men lost at Eyemouth. The women were pulling their men out of the rocks, drowned trying to get into the harbour. But the force of the wind that day, it would blow the sails out of their hands, ye know. They'd have no chance. My grandfather, old Adam Shell, he told me, 'The glass was that low, we didn't go. It was that low, right down below 28.' If we ever saw the glass below 28 again, we never went to sea, ever since those days.

And the lifeboat was run out at the Snook Point – number two lifeboat – ye'll maybe have seen the ruins? George Kyle was the Coxswain in those days. When the wind came, the boat blew up aheight, and they never saw it again. Been a terrible wind. Sudden. Aye.

RH

Fawcuses Drowned, Beadnell, 31st January 1885

There's a headstone to them in the churchyard. I had never seen it; we were told we hadn't to gan in. Old Weir had been with them on the boat; he was one of the crew. And he shoved the pellet up his jumper, and I divvin't know how he was picked up, but he was. And his father, Andrew, and the three sons – Thomas, Robert and Andrew – they were all drowned. Polly's sister's son was called after them, with all those names.

MF

There was more than one lot of Fawcuses lost. They got a little sail. And they'd carry this sail as long as they were able to stop on the water for wind. And some of them told them, 'Divvin't be sae daft!' And it came a lot of wind from the southart. They set the sail about the Middle Bank. Well, my old grandfather was watching. He says, 'He'll not come far with that sail.' Too much sail, ye see. Ah! They were gone! And my grandfather and them went away from the Square. And they put a right night in looking for them. My grandfather and his brother, and old Dick Hall who was drowned at the trouting – they all went. I forget who they all were. They put an awful night in. But ye see, they had had too much sail. Ye cannot be too careful at the sea. The sea's never been beat yet, nor he never will. Never will.

CD

The Blizzard, 6th February 1895

I've told ye about the blizzard? Just what we heard. My father and them were there. They were just young. They were at what Seahouses men call the Off Bank – it was the Bratting Ground. Beadnell men always used to gan there to catch the brats. And that's where they shot the lines.

Oh, they put an awful day in. It was an awful day from the south-east. Just a gale of wind. Our lot shot into it. And the first sea that hit them, they lost the two long oars overboard. There were four oars, ye see, them days. One oar come ashore at this Point, and one come ashore at Seahouses Point the next morn. And my father – he had a cloth or a scarf or something around his head for toothache. And the first sea that landed, it went! He lost that and all!

Now – whae, they just had to gan. Couldn't make nowt of it. They just had to let the boat gan stern first, and keep bailing out. And when they saw the big seas coming, they hoyed the sail over, ye know, to stop her from gaa'n ower-hard. My Uncle Tom, he just sat forrard, and when he saw a great big'un coming he hoyed the sail over, for to dreg her. The boat was full of water. They had to keep bailing out. They had airboxes in, mind, or else they would have went down.

Now, they reckon ye could break the fish through that day, it was that frost.

A coble enters Seahouses harbour under sail, circa 1900.

There was a boat come in about the Benty here, I've heard them say, and they launched the boat for to gan and tell them where they were; they were lying below the Stead. And they couldn't keep the oars on, for the ice on the thowelds.

It was getting on in the afternoon, varnigh dark, when the storm must have cleared a bit. They had gone over the Knivestone, somewhere, our lot. And my uncle Bill – 'O,' he says, 'there's the top of the light,' he says, away south of them. And they got to the Longstone. There were a few boats in at the Longstone, and they got there and all.

They didn't know each other! Their beards were all ice. Aye, and there were two drowned at the Burn that day. Aye. It was an awful day. O aye! An awful day!

CD

Jane Douglas 933 BK, at the Farne Islands, circa 1900. Charlie Douglas' grandfather and his three sons were seven or eight miles offshore when they were caught in the blizzard of 1895. The Seahouses coble Guiding Star was lost in the same storm.

A sailing coble takes visitors past Longstone, circa 1900. The Jane Douglas was the last boat to reach the Islands in the blizzard.

Lifeboat Came in with a Bare Mast

We were two hours into the sea, ye know, easterly wind and rain. And we broke lines that day. We said, 'We'll have to get away in!' But we hauled a little bit more, a little bit more, till we got them. Then we come away.

Well, the last boat to come into Seahouses that day was one o'clock. They say there were no more boats could run in, because it was bad. And the lifeboat was out. They said: 'There's no boat will come in now.'

We come in, thick in the evening. We saw the buoy, North Sun'land – come right up to her, ye know. The seas were breaking across Seahouses! But we got in. And old Geordie Fawcus told me, the lifeboat ran in with a bare mast that day. They came in here (Beadnell) and I can mind, they took the lifeboat back by the road that night. They come in with the bare mast – no sail. So that'll tell ye what wind there was.

CD

The Glass Tells No Lies

Did ye gan in worse weather than they do now? Damn likely! Ye had to gan, ye know, or ye had to hunger. The old men, they studied the glass, ye know.

Now, I'll tell ye something. When the War was on, they were at the sea one day, clock calm. Not a breath of wind. But the glass! It come down. Next morning – still dropping! 'O, we're no gaa'n!' None of the boats went. It was as fine a day as ever shone. But mind, in the darkening, at night! Yes! The wind and the snow – they were there. It come straight away, mind: one crack! Aye, it quick comes, ye know. The glass tells no lies.

CD

Deed Man Bite

Olden days, ye know, shipwrecks and bodies came ashore. A fella at Seahouses, I canna mind his name, he was always going along the sand, to see if there were any bodies. He'd look in their pockets, to see if there was any money. So one morning a fisherman went along ahead of him. He lay down. This fella comes along, looks in his pockets – and he bit him! Ooh, y' bugger! 'Deed man bite! Deed man bite!' He off! And he ran along to Seahouses! 'Deed man bite!'

CD

An anxious moment. The crew of William and R. Archbolds' Lady Fanny Marjoribanks 958 BK, tries to raise the mast on a poor day off Craster, circa 1900. The men on the rocks have thrown a rope to her to try to pull her around.

A steamship ashore at Craster: probably the Worms, 1907.

Rocket Brigade

There was a trawler came ashore at Beadnell, called her the *Sir Edward Grey*. Now, that boat came ashore in 1914. And the skipper asked what part of the main he was on. And my Uncle Jack told him. He said, 'If ye had

been three degrees farther west ye'd have been in my back kitchen.'

Now we took those men out, the Rocket Brigade: 14 men, 14 minutes. That was going some! That was the breeches buoy. That was from when they landed the first one to when they landed the last one. Of course, it would be more than 14 minutes busy, ye know, for to get the gear ready. But from when they started to land the first man till they were all ashore, 14 men, 14 minutes. Now, there was a laddie born at the farm that morning. And they called him Eddie Grey.

JH

Dick Hall and his son William, Drowned Beadnell, 2nd July 1921

Ye see, my father was lost at sea – 1921. And Willy was lost at sea. Both lost together. And we got Father, but we never got Willy. Willy's there yet.

JH

Dick Hall at Beadlin – that was my Uncle Skee Hall's brother. Beautiful morning, month of July. Just one of these things. A wave struck. Old Dick was drowned. His son Willy was never seen. And Freddy with the iron (brace) on his foot was OK. That was the three of them.

JW

It was a Saturday morning, at the nets. Back of the Carrs, Beadnell Bay. And they were pulling across the Carrs. And there was sea coming in. I divvin't know – they must have been ower-far in; but she was a poor boat, mind, a little bit tin thing. Ye see, old Dick, he wasn't drowned. If ye drown ye'll gan to the bottom. But Dick was floating. And Willy – Willy was a good swimmer. But ye see, with the seaboots on, he was lost. And they never got him yet.

CD

Dick Hall and his brother Jack, circa 1950. Their father and brother were drowned at the trout nets on a calm day in Beadnell Bay, 2nd July 1921.

Right: A poster advertising a British Legion Night to raise funds after the loss of the coble Provider, Craster, Friday 10th February 1928. Thomas 'Tombolin' Archbold, James Sanderson and William 'Winker' Stephenson all drowned.

Craster Disaster, 10th February 1928

Well, it was a poor day. They were line-fishing in the month of February; and I can just remember it. I would only be eight years old. My father and them came ashore, and I can remember him saying, 'Where's the *Provider*?' He says, 'It doesn't look ower-good for that boat. They should've been here by now, because they were close to us while we were working the lines.'

And my father and them went back. Just them, ye know. None of the other boats. And I'll tell you, it was some dirty day; a gale of southerly wind, gradually veering south-west and freshening. And all they got floating was a bit of woodwork, a wooden swull and a man's cap. They couldn't stop in the *Our Girls* very long because the weather was deteriorating.

They reckon it was a strong south-east wind, and it drew around about to the sou'west, I can remember that. The boat must have run away on a sea, ye know, and broached-to and turned over – come broadside on to the wave as it was running in front of it. They'll not run straight, a coble. They're dangerous running in front of the wind. They generally tend to come to one side. And it's come to one side and turned over.

And that was my uncle, one of the ones that was killed.

BS

PLAYHOUSE, ALNWICK.

THURSDAY, MARCH 1st, at 7-30.

:-: THE :-:

ALNWICK BRITISH LEGION NIGHT

In aid of the

CRASTER DISASTER FUND.

William R. Stephenson.

James Sanderson.

W. Dawson, T. Grey, R. Archbold, Ralph Archbold, M. Archbold, A. Archbold,
Thos. A. Archbold.

Above is a group of Craster fishermen, of whom Thomas A. Archbold (on extreme right) was drowned.

PROGRAMME.

1.—The Alnwick British Legion Quartette.
2.—GEO. RITCHIE, Baritone.
3.—FRED ADAMSON, Vocalist.
4.—LITTLE MARY ALLAN, Toe Dancer.
5.—F. S. TARELLI, Baritone.
6.—SEP. MOIR, Tenor.
7.—TOM FORSTER, Comedy Entertainer.

8.—TOM MURRAY, Bass.
9.—JACK AND LILY CURRY, Conjuring Entertainment.
10.—Pathe Super Gazette.
11.—An Ideal Comedy.
12.—John Bowers and Anne Cornwall in "THE RAW COUNTRY."

PRICE TWOPENCE.

The Northern Press Ltd., Alnwick.

Rescue of the Faithful II, 17th-19th November 1962

LS: I remember that day, it was Saturday dinnertime. We were called out. The Seahouses lifeboat, too. It come away northerly wind, hail and snow. We couldn't see the length of the boat. With the wind and the hail and the snow, we had to come up here – we lay aback of the Farne Islands there. The Seahouses lifeboat was there – they know all about the Islands, ye know. They were sheltered there. And ye were cold, ye were damp and exhausted. The helicopter come and lifted them off, onto the Farnes. Seahouses lifeboat and all. We went into the lighthouse, Inner Farne. Me and Jimmy Walker. There was a stove. Well, ye couldn't get warm with it. When ye opened the door and poked it, it went out! O, what a time we had! What was it they called the boat?

AR: Tommy Hall's *Faithful*, wasn't it? Tommy was a fella, he wasn't like anybody else. And he went out that day, and it was a poor day, and he hung on and hung on until he couldn't get anywhere. He tried Beadlin first. He couldn't get in here. So he had to go and lie under the Farne. Well, they put the lifeboat out. But it was ower-bad to get back in. So the Holy Island boat came to see if they could be of assistance. They'd just as well have bidden where they were, because they couldn't get back into Holy Island. One of the lads in the fishing boat had a heart condition and he had to be lifted ashore with the helicopter. That would be about the first thing that the helicopter would be used for.

LS: Whae, aye! There was, like, a big bomber come, and he dropped the floating buoys for them to get out by. We were there from Saturday to the Monday, I think.

Jimmy Walker, Second Cox of North Sunderland lifeboat, with his wife Rhoda, 19th November 1962. North Sunderland and Holy Island lifeboats went to the rescue of Faithful II, but all three vessels became stranded in 50 mph gales and heavy seas. The RAF helicopter lifted the men onto the Islands where they stayed for two nights. Fifty-five miles to the south, the Seaham lifeboat was overturned in the same gale, with the loss of nine lives.

The Lifeboat

JW: Two maroons went off for the lifeboat. First one stand-by, the second launch. Ooh aye, they woke ye up alright when the guns went, didn't they, lass? When it was dark at night and quiet, they sounded heavier then.
RhW: There's nobody runs like we used to, when we heard the lifeboat gun! We used to run down to the harbour, but the women doesn't now. They're not fishermen's wives now.

North Sunderland lifeboat Thomas Bewick (1884-1906) at the very end of the 19th century. Coxswain Michael Robson sits aloft. The little girl hiding behind her father, Charlie Dawson, is Tom Dawson's older sister, Anne.

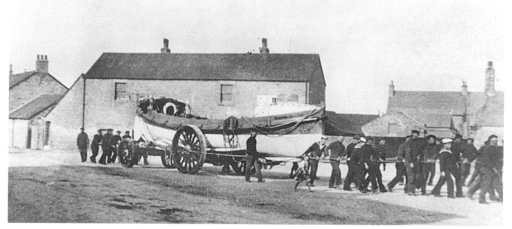

North Sunderland lifeboat, probably the Forster Fawsett (1906-25). The lifeboat house stood on the main road, opposite the present War Memorial. Sail and oar were used to power lifeboats long after most fishing boats had engines. Seahouses did not get its first motor lifeboat until 1936.

JW: Aye, I was in the lifeboat a little few years. Forty-five year, I was in it. Ten year a head-launcher. The two of us did roughly a hundred years.

RhW: I was on the teas – Lifeboat House. Ladies' Guild.

JW: Some were good and ye got a laugh, and others ye didn't. O it was sorrowful to gan to some … Ah, she was alright, though. Your mind was far from being scared, Hin. Ye were looking for life; that's what ye were looking for. I think it was 50 – wasn't it 50, lass? – 50 or 55 lives, I've saved. I've got a plaque from the Institution up the stairs. 50 or 55 lives. And all the years I was in it, I never had a holiday.

RhW: He wouldn't take a holiday!

JW: Mind, all the teer ye get in a lifeboat is a heap of wet clothes. Don't get nowt else. There's nothing to keep ye dry!

Boulmer lifeboat with the women who helped launch her, circa 1920. In 1913 this lifeboat was involved in the rescue of 25 lives from the French steam trawler, Tadorne. The tracks, or 'pedrail', helped transport the boat over sand or snow.

Lifeboat Capsized

According to RNLI records, the First Coxswain who fell overboard during this incident of 28th February 1937 was Thomas Kyle. More than a half century later, at the age of 80, Robin Henderson remembers the story differently:

I've been in the lifeboat when it turned over – 1937. There's only two of us left alive that was in the lifeboat when it capsized. That was a terrible day, that. By gum, some wind that day! How the hell that lifeboat survived that storm I'll never know yet! Well now, we were called out that day, and my father was a Coxswain. I remember old Johnny Markwell was the other one, First Coxswain. My father was Second. My father was steering that day when she upset. He was a fella with a strong character, my father. He was six foot and strong as a horse. And this day, we went down into Berwick Bay. Seas coming along the boat – Look out, they're coming! Crashing along the deck. Looking out below the canopy, watching them coming!

Well, this day – we fired flares. Nothing. No wirelesses in lifeboats those days – no direction-finders and all the paraphernalia. Well, this day we were down there – whether the compass was wrong – ye couldn't steer a course. Ye couldn't see nothing for snow. Just now and again, ye'd see the Longstone flashing there, and out again. And ye're just steering by your local knowledge, really. By gum, we must have been among the shoals, Berwick Bay. There's the Hirst, there's the Towers, there's the Little Beanstackses, the Big Beanstackses – all the old names, Aye. So, among them somewhere, by God, the seas coming down among these shoals. It was just turning light. How the hell we got out in the dark I don't know.

So we were just coming up through the Bay, running. Father says, 'We'll never get in there!' But he says, 'Run the drogue.' So when ye starts running the drogue in the open sea, with the lifeboat – it's only used coming over the Bar. It's like a brake, canvas, a cone. Ye check it, and ye loosen it away. Ye have to have a good team, two or three on each rope.

And Johnny Markwell went overboard. There was a kink in the rope from the boat to the drogue – and Johnny got his foot caught in that. And he was skidding on his behind like that, face to the boat – I could see him yet, being towed with the boat as she went ahead. And old Jack Singleton the engineer, he had a five-gallon drum of waste-oil from the sump. Ye've heard tell of oil on troubled waters? Well, that's the idea of it – it helps keep the swell down. Well, this day, when she upset, when the boat turned over, the lid came off it. It was all over the boat! My father had to take his lifebelt off and stand on it to steer the boat.

And we got him aboard, we got Johnny. Well, when the lid came off, the oil was all over the sea, and I'm sure that's what saved him. We got him aboard.

And the boat we were going to rescue? It was a bloody false alarm!

Sunset, Holy Island. 6964

The Lifeboat House, Holy Island, 1930s. There were two lifeboat stations on the Island. This one was by the Heugh, beneath the Abbey ruins, the other at the Snook. Holy Island had one of the first lifeboats in the country, established in 1802 by the Crewe Trustees. The two stations closed in 1934 and 1968.

World War I

Although fishing was a reserve occupation, many men from the coastal villages went away to serve in both World Wars. From Holy Island alone in World War II, 38 men went away out of a total Island population of 220. The following extracts concentrate mainly on the home front.

In 1913, the year before the outbreak of World War I, Harry Hawker made a first, unsuccessful attempt to fly around the British Isles in his Sopwith sea-plane. He made an unexpected landing in Beadnell Haven on 25th August. Charlie Douglas was four years old and Tom, his brother, seven.

The First Sea-plane

CD: Queer place this, ye know, Beadnell. The first sea-plane to fly round the British Isles – it was in there, all night. In the Haven there. There ye are now. I can remember that same as it was the now.

TD: It'd be afore the First World War. A Sopwith.

CD: He flew round the British Isles. O it would be afore the First War. They were at the herring fishing.

TD: I think I would be seven year old on that day, the 25th August. My birthday. There ye are, now! The boats was at the herring.

CD: We were down the rocks, playing. And it come round the Point there, and I says to wor Tom, 'Hey! Looka yonder! There's a muckle gate come ower the Point end!' 'Cos it looked like a gate, ye know, flying. And they put him into the Haven, where we had the boat moored, the *Lady Elcho*.

TD: They were here from Newcastle and all over on bicycles.

CD: There was hundreds there seeing him.

TD: From Flamborough Head and all over – hey, I'm not joking. They travelled all night, just to see the plane! Aye, a little sea-plane, ye know. He was moored across the Haven there. And he stopped up at Beadnell Hall, at Colonel Craster's. And they bid all night. We watched him gan away the next morning. Aye. I can mind of that fine.

CD: Mind, I was very little.

The First Aeroplane

I remember the first aeroplane we'd ever seen – First World War. We were swinging in the boat shed as boys, three or four of us. All of a sudden there was a stampede. There was an aeroplane – two – going about looking for submarines, I would think. And it dropped down. Engines cut out. The other fella landed in the field up there. And he reported his pal had landed in the sea. They went away with the boat – no engines then, oars and sail – and they got him, sitting straddle-legged across the plane, and brought him back. We were all out watching the other fella take off. The women were running like hell when he roared up the field; they were falling down, getting their long skirts in a tangle, the roar of it like a monster coming upon them. They ran like hell!

Aye, I can remember the First World War. I can remember going up to the Church, Sunday nights, with my mother – she would be young then. Run like hell! In the dark, running home. 'Come on, ye have to run! The Germans will be getting ye!'

Old Sally Cromarty that had the shop – she was a widow. And she had a son lost in the First World War. Aye, George Cromarty. His name's on the plaque in the Church. And I remember that day. I was out at the farm, Sunday morning, I'd be seven, or eight coming up, and I was talking to the farmer, giving him the message that George Cromarty had been killed in France. Terrible days, when ye think about them.

RH

An unidentified airship, probably British, over Seahouses during World War I. Pat Laidler recalls German Zepplins, en route to Edinburgh during that War, dropping flares on Seafield Farm and setting the haystacks on fire.

British submarine G-11 wrecked in fog near Howick, 22nd November 1919. Two crewmen died in the incident.

German Submarines

I can remember when the First World War started. There were two of our boats out fishing, and there was a submarine on top of the water – he couldn't submerge. The warship came down from the Tyne and sunk it. And there was a big ship ashore at Bamburgh, what they called the *Tredegar Hall*. That was the First World War. But ye didn't know there was a War on. The War was in France and them places.

But then the Second World War, 'it was all over ye. Civilians were mixed up in it just as much as the Army and Navy was.

JW

Ellen Stephenson of Boulmer, aged 18, helped dismantle the submarine at Howick. The wood in this photograph, however, suggests that here she might be working on another shipwreck.

German Submarine Sighting, 8th June 1915

O aye, I've seen some queer things here. I'll tell ye what I've seen: I've seen a Garman submarine, firing at a steamboat – there ye are now.

First World War; we were at the harbour on a Saturday morning. I'd be very little. And I can mind the same as it was the now: I think it was my father and them, and I think they were shooting creeves. Sailing days, ye know. And Wooh! A right thud to the south-east. Oh! A big steamboat went down. Mind, she was a big boat. Submarine sunk her.

Now, that night, it was light, maybes about 6 o'clock time. And there was another steamboat coming north, close in. Whae, the submarine come up – we could see him. About the Middle Bank tack, where the boats fish yonder – firing at him! Ye could see the shots hitting the water! He never hit him, but he was getting close, mind. He was coming right into the rock-ends, the steamboat.

And there was a trawler, a minesweeper, went away from the Farne House – he must have been at the light. And he followed him. And he was firing at him. But ye see, the submarine would dive. They hadn't the gadgets to tell then.

Now, old Ned Gallifer was in that boat, belonging Seahouses. That's old Hannah's brother; Jimmy Walker's uncle.

Now, I think that's the same submarine, mind, that wor lot reported. I divvin't know much about it. I just know that they were at the sea one day, and wor old man says, 'What the damn's that?' A telegraph post gaa'n through the water! It was a periscope, ye know. Just the top of it. And they come and reported it. And that night, the destroyers come up from the Tyne. And they reckon he come up in front of one and he never stopped. 'Wuff!' Cut him right through the middle. Aye.

I think it was a hundred quid they got for reporting it.

CD

Old Hannah

There was an old woman here, old Hannah, Skee Hall's wife. She had been to the herring at Yarmouth. So when the First War broke out she says, 'Steen,' – that was wor old grandfather: 'Is Yarmouth on wor side?'

'Aye!'

She says, 'We're alright, then!'

So – 'What's the news this morning, Steen?'

He says: 'The Dutch has captured Holland! Setten fire to 20 mile of sea!'

'Eeh, the buggers, Steen! The buggers!'

They would tell her owt!

CD

Old Steen – Stephens – lived on the corner of Beadnell Square. The old man had a beard; I can just remember him and his wife, old Mary Ann. And of course Hannah had been out on the bank edge this morning. The War was on, and she was aye looking to see if there were any naval boats went past, 'cos Uncle Tom was an only son, ye see. And she was worried stiff when he was away. They were all away at the War. Dad was in the minesweepers and so was Uncle Tom. And she used to be out looking for them.

So when Steen says, 'The Germans have setten fire to the North Sea!' she'd be crying into her pinny, worrying about Uncle Tom.

MF

World War II

Start of World War II

The War started on the Sunday, and on the Monday, the next day, mind – it was a poor day, northerly wind and rain – we were all standing at the hut corner, and here's a plane come by, right low down. Wor Tom had the gun. I said, 'If that had been a Garman … !' Whae, it was! Great Garman plane! He dropped a bomb about Scremerston, I think. But right low down! Aye! Aye! We saw by the thing on the side that he was a Garman, just when he went close by.

CD

Above: A string of herring, Main Street, Seahouses, August 1937. The Evening Chronicle headline: 'Russia and Germany Invited to … Talk.' Below: Anxious news around the time of the outbreak of World War II: visitors on Harbour Road, Beadnell, summer 1939.

Mines

When this War was on there was any amount of mines come ashore. Ye had to get a permit at the finish to gan on the beach to get bait. They were all ower. I can mind the first mine was ablow the huts there at the Square. And ye know, everybody that touched it got bad hands. Then there was a one off Collith. It wasn't right in – 200 or 300 yards off the shore, easterly wind. It was about dinnertime. I was standing watching it. Blue flash and such a crack. I divvin't know what he touched, but he went up.

There was a mine come ashore at the Stead and all. One of the laddies was gaa'n to take the horns off! Went away for spanners!

One night about tea-time we were coming in from the lines. There was a fella standing on the Point, waving us into the harbour. Whae, the tide wasn't right. It was no good. There was a mine right in here, where we launch the boats down at the Benty. It had come right in through the narrow opening. Well, how the hell it got through there … !

CD

Lt-Gen Sir Ronald Adam, Chief of the Northern Command, and his Staff, inspect defences at Beadnell harbour, World War II.

Women's War Work

I was called up. I went to the training estate at Gateshead, to train to be a fitter. They said, 'O, ye can go into the Land Army ... ' I says, 'I'm not going onto no land! I want to see the world!' Aye! And away I goes.

I remember going as plain as it was yesterday. We went to the training estate for three month; and I turned out to be very good with my hands. I remember the foreman saying, 'What have ye been doing? Have ye worked with this sort of thing before?' And I said 'No.' I could go to a thousandth of an inch with the ratchet screwdriver, no problem. Anyway, we were posted to Rugby making bombers. And mind, we did widen our horizons in Rugby. O, aye!

MD

Harry Tait's Navy

I was away for five and a half year in the Navy – what we called Harry Tait's Navy, the minesweepers. Stephen Douglas joined up with me.

A very big percentage of the young men from here (Holy Island) had to go to War – there were only one or two old ones left. My father was one, and he went to the sea himself for quite a while. So the fishing, with the five or six years of the War, built up. The quantities of lobsters and crabs recovered a lot.

RW

Stephen was away on Atlantic Patrol. Whae, he was all over the world. We were married in St Andrew's Church in Rugby on 22nd April 1942. I had the twins, 23rd June 1943. And Stephen came home from America the night before the twins were born. He left when they were four days, and he never saw them till they were two and a half. So when I hear these lot moaning, their man was away a fortnight – well, ye've got something to say, haven't ye?

MD

Requisitioning

Now, as he was getting older, Dad decided to gan in for a bigger boat. I was working at the time, so I'm not very sure if it was Dad's boat completely, or whether he shared with Mr Dixon ('Young Punch'). But I reckon Dad would be skipper of that boat. They called her the *Dewy Rose*. When I was married in '38, she would be about two year old then. She was built at Harrison's.

Then the government came. I divvin't know just when in the War, but it was pretty early on. And the government came when they come in from the sea one Saturday, and told them to take out their fishrooms and oars and things. They had to take the boat to Blyth, on a Saturday afternoon. It went away on a wagon on the Monday. There were 20-something cobles, a whole lot, all on wagons. They got something for them, but it wasn't very much. And that was three men's wages.

She came back. She came to Amble, 'cos she was built there, ye see. Dad took me and Arthur down to see her one Sunday. We didn't know what we were going to see. He says, 'Get into her.' She was lying on the brae. And we got into her. And I says to Dad at the finish, 'She's not the *Dewy Rose*, this?' He says, 'Aye. That's what they've sent back. That's what I've to go back to sea in.' He says, 'Ye could read the papers through her planks.'

He never went to sea in her again. He sold her, but I divvin't know who bought her.

MF

Beadnell Bay, August 1938. Geordie Fawcus in the Dewy Rose BK 173, one of many cobles later to be requisitioned for War use. Next to him in the small boat, Seagull, is the author's father, aged nine.

Longstone Bombed

CD: I saw the plane when he bombed the Longstone.

TD: We saw him! We saw him dinnertime! He just went around and around, daylight! Dinnertime, wasn't it? I tell ye – there used to be a Garman plane went by here as regular as the 5 o'clock bus!

CD: Garmans was always gaa'n fleeing about there, woman. I can mind, he flew round about and he dropped one at the Longstone. Ye could see the bomb come down – Whooh! The house that the foghorn was in – he put them into yon hole, the back side. But the light wasn't hit, mind. Just a flash, and a crack! And the things were down as he hit her. Aye!

TD: Whae aye! Yes, that's right. O, and there's been Garman prisoners in here many a time, in the hut. Whae, the lads were right enough. They were stationed up here, prisoners. The cheekiest soldiers were the Londoners. They had more to say than anybody!

Bomb damage to the foghorn of Longstone Lighthouse. Three bombs were dropped from a German He 111 bomber on the afternoon of Friday, 1st August 1941 and two made direct hits on the turret and engine room.

CD: O aye, there were a lot a soldiers in here during the War.

TD: O the Garmans were quiet. They never said owt to me.

CD: They were getting the barbed wire down along the beach. They were alright.

TD: They were nice enough fellas.

The Patia, 27th April 1941

The month of April 1941 I was aboard a minesweeper out of North Shields. We used to sweep from Hartlepool to about four miles off the Longstone or vice versa. We were sweeping this night, very dark. I was on the gun platform on watch when I saw firing astern of us – tracers going into the sky. The next thing was this sheet of flame in the sky which hurtled into the sea. We thought, rightly as it turned out, that the ship had shot the plane down. We heard shortly after that the plane had put a bomb right down the ship's funnel, sinking her, and was immediately shot down itself. We pulled our sweeps in and were told to lie where we were till daylight. There was near a mutiny aboard our ship that night. 'Why don't we go and see if we can't get any survivors?' But no, we had to stay where we were.

One trawler (minesweeper) was allowed, or ordered, to go. That was the *Chassiron*. He launched his small boat at the scene, and in charge of the boat was Jimmy Carrs, a fisherman who was in the Navy like me. He came from Boulmer. I knew him well. They went to a rubber float, and who should be in it but the three German airmen from the He 111 that had sunk the ship.

I wonder if any of them are still alive? I don't know any more about what went on or if they got any survivors; but I do know, come daylight, when we went to the scene, I saw a sight I do not ever wish to see again.

There were bodies floating everywhere. A lot could have been saved, had we been allowed to go back straight away. All the men had lifebelts on. Some were in floats but all had perished with the cold. We picked up a raft with three men, all stokers, just in their trousers. Two would be in their 40s, the other was just a boy, maybe 15-16. One of the older fellows had the young lad cradled in his arms, their heads together, trying to comfort the young lad. They died like that. All three had been badly scalded. Our group leader should have been hung, drawn and quartered. They nearly had to get the armed patrol in when we got ashore. Some of our crew wanted to shoot him.

Now they called that ship the *Patia*, a new reconditioned armed merchant cruiser out of the Tyne. We were doing a sweep down the buoyed channel to make sure it was clear of mines. And later, we fished close to that wreck with out greatlines.

BS

Like many fishermen, Bill Smailes served in the Navy during World War II. He witnessed the sinking of the aircraft catapult ship, HMS Patia, bombed by a German aircraft off Boulmer on 27th April 1941. Thirty nine men were killed. The Boulmer lifeboat took part in the rescue.

Minesweeper HMT Inchgower. Many British trawlers were converted to minesweeping duties in World War II.

HEARTH AND HOME

THE VILLAGE, HOLY ISLAND 6157

Fiddler's Green, Holy Island, circa 1900. Bent grass was used to thatch houses at one time – as appears to be the case with the white house near the centre of this picture.

Housing

I can remember the old houses. Old fishermen like old George Douglas, they had the beds in there – ye'll maybe have seen them? Box beds. Cleverly made, ye know. Any of the women that was going to have a new arrival in the family, ye left your home, ye away to your grandfather's for the night. I can see him yet, Old Adam Shell, white beard. Used to wear tiddleywink hats, little hats with a bit tassle on. I used to get in behind him for bed, 'cos there was no room really. I'd be six or seven years old, lying behind him. Along the wall, there'd be two beds, curtains along; and they were nicely-shaped, fancy. And if she'd had a boy or a girl in the night they would say, 'Aye, Henderson's got a little boy down in the Mussel Hole this morning!' Aye. Kid ye up, ye know.

RH

They used to thatch their houses. I cannot remember it, but they did. They thatched their houses here with bents. The simple reason is that there's an area here that was supposedly for thatching. And the long bent is just as good as what ye would go and grow elsewhere. It's workable and it's strong.

RW

Hooky Mats

My mother used to say to my sister Evelyn, 'Ye've got a tongue would clip cloots!' They all used to make the hooky mats. Hook them out. Everybody used to help making the mats for the winter. When the summer finished: 'Somebody wants a mat made!' All the girls would join together, half a dozen or seven or eight of them get round, and they had it made in no time. They used to make them with pieces of cloth and all, pieces of clipping. Lovely, aye.

I can remember when my mother had a new one made. It was just grand, snuggling, that warm, ye know, beside the kitchen fire. Father would come in with his ducks – he'd been to the swad, out on the slakes there, winter nights; laid them around the fire there, the dog lying at the side. And he'd be cleaning the gun; and the ducks – he'd wash them in the basin, wash all the mud off them. It was good to see them nice and clean again. And me lying there on the mat, playing with them, flipping their feet!

RH

Beadnell Square

There's the Square. Ye're gaa'n back a bit now. They sometimes kept their gear in the middle there, the men. And there was nettles and brambles and all things growing on the inside. You could look through our bedroom windows into the Square at the back. It was quite wild, but a lot of the men had gear in.

They seemed to have big lofts in them, the middle ones. Our bedrooms was all in the lofts. Whae aye! We had like stoothin' walls. Some of the lofts had proper walls. Possibly they had made them a bit better by then. But I think some of them at one time just had sails up. Bits of sails they weren't using.

They had a pantry in under the stairs. And we had a nice big bedroom upstairs. O, quite warm. There was just the one fire. They kept nice big fires on. They had to – the women had all the bait to skeyn in front of them. Now, it was a rough life.

The netties were where ye went down the banks. Ye know where the breakwater is, farther along? Well, they were on the bank top afore ye gan

Beadnell Square, built 1777, stood just south of the black huts on Harbour Road. In 1851 it had 48 residents in its 11 cottages. Jack Hall and Tom and Charlie Douglas were born here.

down onto the breakwater. I hated to gan to Aunt Lizzie's! Because, mind, at any time there could have been a landslide and that netty would be away!

MF

Water

The water was all to carry. Have ye heard tell of Colonel Craster? Well, there was a tap right opposite the road at their gate. And it was all to carry from there. And there wasn't always water in that tap. When there wasn't water in that tap, ye had to go to what they called the Vicarage Pump. And there was a proper – well, it was like a spring in there. That was never dry. There was always plenty of water there. That was right up in the plantation, that. Ye could always get water there, but ye couldn't always get it at the tap.

At the Benty, they got their water out the well. It was all built up, with a tap on it. The Allhusens were the first'uns to get water in the house (Beadnell Towers). They were Newcastle people, in textiles, I think.

JH

For water, ye went to the village pump. That was in Bamburgh, but in Beadnell it would be the same. Even before we went to school, we used to have to carry the water, with the 'gerrards' around and the pails. We said a 'gerrard' – it was just a hoop. It lay on the pails so that the water didn't splash ye.

MD

All the water had to be carried from the well in buckets, ye know. What they called a 'gerd', a square wood one; and ye could just carry them by the handles and it wouldn't come against you, with the gerd round you. Aye. And most of the young lads and girls sweethearted down at the well there. The lads carried the water up for them.

RH

Craster south side, circa 1900. Washing dries outside the Jolly Fisherman inn, at this time owned by Mr Fortune. The barrels lined up are of herring, not beer.

Electricity

It would be afore the War (World War II) when we got the electric here. The first light in Beadnell, it was at the Benty. What we call the Bent Hall down there where we haul the boats up, ye know. There was a big light on there, for when ye gan down at night to pull the boats up or launch them down the morn. It was a grand affair; they were litten up. That was about the first light in Beadnell. Then after that we got them at the harbour and different places.

CD

Hygiene

Maybe a lot of them'll not like to hear it now, but it's the truth: the old places weren't a very clean place, till everything was modernised. Because, ye know, everything was tipped over the banks. All the slops and everything. Dishes and all things. Everything they didn't want was hoyed over the banks. There was a sewer went down along about Patterson's garage somewhere, and all. And everybody's toilet, what went into the pails, had to be buried. But ye'd always get somebody that wasn't all that particular. When we got to the village, my dad used to bury it in the gardens. When it was ash pits, the men used to come and clean the ash pits out. It was Kennedys, when the Kennedys was in the farm.

MF

We whitewashed everything. The wash-house. The coal-house! Eeh, we just made work for ourselves! Mother even used to whitewash where the pan went for the cinders under the grate. We blackleaded the range, with the pot on one side and the oven on the other; then she whitewashed where the cinders went. I can see her yet, on her hands and knees, with the playgen jar – the ware jar, playgen, we called it, a big two-pound clay jar – full of whitewash, slapdashing it on, and the cinders falling down from the fire and fizzing. We used to mix the whitewash up in the jar. It come as a sort of powder, and ye had to add water. And everything was done every year. And every year we spring-cleaned

110

Low Newton before World War I. Rainwater for washing is collected from the roof in barrels. This card is postmarked 1914.

the front room, we washed the handle of the broom and the duster, and all the garden tools – the spade and the grape and the hoe. We just made work!

MB

Diseases and Cures

Ye only have to read the old school minutes: it shows you exactly how things have changed. Completely. The old school – they were either off school with scarlet fever or chicken pox or whatever there was, and diphtheria, all this sort of thing; and they weren't at school from August till the end of October, because they were at the herring; and then it was the harvest and the potatoes. The older people – the majority of women, if ye walk up to the cemetery – they're 34, 35; and a baby that died in childbirth. The babies up in that cemetery, they're unbelievable.

MD

Ye know what they call the Malley Stairs in Seahouses? Ye know as ye go through the Nick, the stairs down to the bottom? Well, I've no idea who Malley was, but that's always been the Malley Stairs. And ye go down the Malley Stairs, and ye're going away to the left, and the first house on the left was Andrew Rutter's Uncle Bob. Then there was Andrew, his Aunt Thomasin, his Uncle Jack and his Uncle Harry, and his Aunt Bel. There were five cottages. The whole family was together.

Old Jack, he was 90-odd when he died. Jack never was in hospital in his life. He wasn't married, he never had a doctor in his life, never had been to a dentist, and he smoked a pipe all his life. There was one day at the fishing in the *Regina* – it was before Andrew's day. Andrew's Uncle Danny Allen went away with Jack. And they were hauling the gear, just at the North Buoy there; they were on with crab pots.

Now, it happened pretty often. Ye had to watch what ye were doing. The rope would make a full turn on the hauler – what we call a 'riding' – and it would take it in from both ends. And ye had to watch, 'cos your hand was

Fishermen's cottages, The Nick, Seahouses, early 1900s.

straight in. I've been in a hauler once. Once is plenty! Well, Jack's hand got in and it took the finger-end off. 'Oh,' he says; 'It'll feed a codling!' He flipped it overboard. They wrapped a bit twine around about it. Hardy old boys!

PL

RhW: He had an auntie, she lived till she was a hundred, and nine month. And she made some lovely salve. Black salve, we called it. O, she wouldn't tell ye what was in it. And she gave it to her granddaughter, but they couldn't make it like her.
JW: Three parts on it was red lead.
RhW: Aye, and home-fed lard.
JW: And all like that.
RhW: He used to gan to her.
JW: I used to gan to her with a bad hand.
RhW: And she used to wash them and dress your hand. We used to wash our hands with alum – put a little bit alum into the water, and it took all the soreness out your hands.
JW: And I'll tell ye what they used a lot on the old hands and that. Poultices. Linseed poultices. And oatmeal poultices.
RhW: But they dinna get the bad wrists like they used to get.
JW: No, no. It was the hard oilskins what did that; scraping around your wrist all the time.
RhW: They used to get terrible boils on their wrists.
JW: And once ye got a dose of the boils, ye never got clear on them.
RhW: We used to like the red flannel bandages for to put on their wrists. Used to wrap them round, then wash them every night. Stopped the chafe of the oilskins. It kind of helped.

Old Dr Macaskie used to come from Bamburgh in the horse and trap. We never had him. Except when Mother was ill – and then she probably didn't have him, it probably would be the district nurse, or the next door neighbour. When Mother died she was only 59.

Mother was a great hand with different concoctions. I couldn't tell ye what they were! Ye got them rammed down ye! Cod-liver oil or olive oil – anything oily. Scott's Emulsion! Ugh! That was the cure-all end-over-all! That's supposed to cure everything! The fella standing with the fish on the bottle! The fisher-people used to get goose-grease rubbed on their chests. I divvin't think it did them any good! Mind, my husband's father was 93, and the uncle was 91.

MD

Dentist

I'd been having toothache for a while. But you know what it's like getting them out. It was a hundred times worse then!

'Bill, come here. I want you.'

'What y' want, Da?'

'Come to the front room and see! It's aa'right. Come on!'

I was grabbed; pushed into the sitting room. Oh God! I was sure it was the devil himself standing there in a black suit, with a great muckle silver squirter in his hand. I know it was a squirter, because he gave it a squeeze and this brown liquid came out the end. It was a hollow needle, thick as the blunt end of a darning needle. I know I started squalling. Says I: 'But he's not putting that thing in ma mooth!'

Vividly I remember. I relaxed a bit and Dad let go of me. I ducked and out of that door like a bat out of hell. They never found me for the rest of that day.

BS

Front Street, Sea Houses.

Main Street, Seahouses, looking west, circa 1910. Coxon's Drapers (right) has a window full of toy boats. Left of it is Turnbull's grocery store, later Kilbourne's, and Scott's the butcher. Travelling dentist 'Chin-Chin' Atkinson had his surgery upstairs.

Shops

Thomas Simpson who was drowned in the pond had two sisters, and they had the little shop which was the only shop there was in Beadnell then. Bread and butter, and whatever ye wanted, ye would get it there. When ye went for half an ounce of baccy, they had a mark on the counter to cut it.

There was a shop at the old Square, and there was a one at the village. Now, the one at the village was right opposite the Church. Summers had it. And that was the shop and the post office. The joiner's shop was against the grocer's shop.

There was what they called an off-licence at the Square. That wasn't a pub. Whatever ye were drinking – beer, whisky, whatever it was – ye had to drink that outside. Take a jug down. Take a pail!

I can remember when they built the café in Beadnell, on the roadside yonder (Harbour Road). The lifesaving apparatus used to be on the other side. There was a big house stood on your right as you come down from the Church. It was a branch of the Seahouses Store.

The greengrocer used to come around with a donkey, and what they called a flat. They called him Jack Bell. And he had all his fruit on the flat. So there were two fellas at Beadnell, Charlie Steen was one, and they took the donkey out and put him in the field. And then they pushed the shafts through the gate, and they heuked the donkey into it. The donkey was on one side of the gate and the fruit was on the other!

JH

High Newton post office, early 1900s. Third from right, with beard: Tom Wright. Effie, his daughter, ran the post office. At this time it was possible to send a postcard in the morning and receive a reply by early afternoon.

Harbour Road, Beadnell, August 1933. The shop to the left of the picture, now rebuilt as 'Seabreeze', was an Infirmary Hut on Alnmouth Links during World War I. It was moved to Beadnell as Laidler's shop and café shortly afterwards.

Sally Cromarty's, Holy Island

Old Sally had the shop next to here. She was a great character, was old Sally. We'd walk in her house and she would have her glasses up on her head, ye know, and we'd say: 'What's the matter wi' ye the day, Sally?' And she'd say: 'I'm looking for me glasses! I cannot find them anywhere!' Aye. Old Sally. She had the shop there all my life. Ran it herself before the daughter took it over. A little bit of everything, ye know. If somebody went in and said: 'Have ye got so-and-so, Sally?' – 'Have ye got a needle or have ye got thread?' – 'No, I haven't: but I'll have it tomorrow!' So the next traveller that come in, that was on the order. She'd get, O, little bits of all sorts. But it was mostly sweets. And a few bits of groceries.

O, Sally was open all hours! And the lads and girls used to congregate there in the winter, in her kitchen, where she lived, and sit round about. I've seen dozens sitting in. At night-time, it was just like a meeting-place. And the shop was there if ye wanted anything. And the smoke! The fire smoked like hell!

Aye, she was a lass, was Sally. Monkey-nuts, apples – she would carry so much out the shop onto the table in the winter. Cadbury's selection box – Walnut Whips and things like that were tuppence a bar. And some liked Snowballs, and they were about a ha'penny. One of her favourites was Cowan's Toffee, ye know, with the cow on it. Do ye know what the Islanders always called it when they went into Sally's? 'Let's have a bar of bull's cream!' Now that was tuppence a bar, I think, at that time.

I've seen them sit and talk all night in there. I've seen them sit and play cards, not gambling or anything. Just sit and play whist or whatnot – there was a lot of whist played about here at that time. Then the lads would come in from the duck-shooting, and tell their tales about how many ducks they didn't shoot. No electric light, ye know. All candles or lamps.

RW

Holy Island Riot

Did ye ever hear tell of the Holy Island Riot? Well, there'd been a ship ashore. This was a great place for hiding things when stuff come ashore. There were Customs Men in those days, as well. Well now, there'd been a ship. They must have salvaged it or something – got ship money for it. All the men had gathered at the Crown and Anchor, to share the money. So old Dougal Cromarty came out for his supper. So when he came out, round the corner, the first house he came to was the Policehouse, see. And for devilment, he would knock, and maybe run. Not the door, but the window. Well! He put his fist through it! And the Policeman was just coming out on duty at the very time. He opened the door and he grabbed him. Pulled him in!

Now, just as they pulled him in the door, one of the other men going for his supper come out the Crown and Anchor; and he saw it happen. And he turned back, and he says; 'Ye bugger, that's the Policeman pulled Dougal into the cells!' So they went out. They away down to the beach. They got a great big mast and they knocked the door and windows in. Heave-Ho! Heave-Ho! – with the great big mast. I've heard my mother say, her hair turned snow white that night with fear, for the carry-on there was. The men would all be crazy, shouting with drink. Ye know what they are when they have a share in the ship-money. They couldn't just take the money home to their wives. I don't know how they got it cooled down in the end. Mounted police came over from Berwick. Somebody would have to pay for it, likely. It must have been just afore I was born.

Old Sally told me all about it. Sally Cromarty. She says she was going round the village, walking, a moonlight night, sweethearting – linking, ye know – and saw it all. That's how things is handed down! Aye, they were daft buggers!

RH

Cromarty Bros, Holy Island carriers, at Chare Ends. Though Holy Island seems a peaceful place, it was not always so. Following the wreck of the Shadwan, March 1889, the local Policeman, PC Johnson, served two Islanders with summonses for stealing her cargo. A riot followed, in which several Islanders were charged.

Transport and Industry

Now, Geordie Patterson built a garage on (Beadnell) links. He did something that suited Mrs Craster well. And she gave him a letter that said there was nobody could shift Geordie Patterson off them links.

Jackie Hall had the first motor car that was ever in Beadnell. It was one of them little black ones. We used to call it a pillbox. Jackie got that for £5, second-hand. And there was no licence for cars then. Anybody who could buy a car could get a one. We used to gan all over. We used to gan to Warkworth horse races at one time.

JH

Mother's father was a shepherd with Coxon's up at Swinhoe. Granny used to love us going – she kept her bed aired all the time for us to gan. We push-biked (from Blyth to Beadnell) – three and a quarter hours. We had a tandem as well. We went on a fine night whenever we could, when granny was alone.

MF

Ye got to Wooler sometimes with the Sunday School trip, with the horse and trap. Ye got to Berwick once a year, on Berwick Fair Saturday. Sixpence for the ticket, or ninepence, from Beal station, along to Berwick and back again. Changed days. There's no station there now. And the buses and coaches come in by their thousands.

Olden days, ye didn't know what was going on in the world. Ye had your own way of life. Ye made your own fun. There was a reading room at the entrance to the village. Ye went along and read the papers. Then they came on, wirelesses and what have ye. It was just before the War really, ye know.

I was keen on the football in my young days. I played on the teams on the mainland there. Aye, the winter-time, Saturdays, ye'd come across the sands – terrible weather. Horse and cart – or run across. And ye would go to Beal in the charabanc; pick the team up and away into the country!

RH

North Sunderland Railway, early 1920s. The station was on the site of the present main carpark. The line ran to Chathill. The loco 0-6-0 tank engine Bamburgh was known locally as 'the Tankie'.

There was a surprising amount of industry other than fishing along the coast in the 18th to early 20th century. Seahouses and Beadnell harbours were built to serve the grain and lime industries, and Craster was famous for its whinstone quarries, which operated until World War II. Below: Norwell Brow Quarry, Craster.

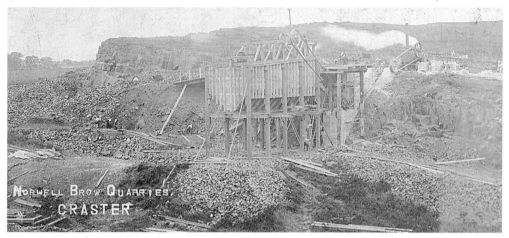

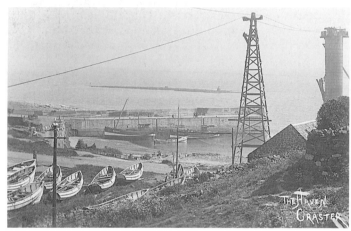

Left: The aerial flight from Craster quarry to the harbour.

Below: Loading a stone boat at 'the Bins', Craster south pier, circa 1910. The Bins were dismantled in 1939, as they were thought to be a potential navigational mark for enemy aircraft during World War II.

Entertainments

A charabanc outing beside the Craster Arms, Beadnell, 1920s.

Seahouses Feast

There was a Feast in all the villages. O aye. Ye started in Berwick, ye come to Seahouses, ye carried on to Beadnell, to Newton, to Craster; ye carried on to Amble. Ye went to them all. Well, maybe not to Amble. Seahouses Feast was in the market square yonder. Close to the 12th or the 15th of August. Now, Beadlin was six weeks after that. That was the end of the year for them. The shows were here. Ye had the hobby-horses (roundabout). And then ye had the hoopla, ye had coconut shies, ye had shuggy boats. Shooting. O, aye! It was a great night. And then there were stalls came with fruit on. Not so many sweets, mostly fruit.

JW

Boulmer Feast

The villages weren't that big enemies. They always gathered at the Feast. On Boulmer Feast – the first Monday in July, wasn't it? – ye had your sports day and the gypsies used to come with their donkeys. And they used to have races for the boats and whatnot. And ye always used to invite some of your neighbours – the Craster men, and Hauxley, because Amble wasn't a fishing village. And in them days, ye always killed two 'Ministers' (curly-tailed animals) for bacon. And ye boiled a ham for the feast, and ye had a real set-to, ye know. Boiled ham and peas and peas-pudding! O we had some right dos!

GS

They had a concert up there one time, at the hut. Laugh! John Allan and all them lot, and old Bill Liddell. Get him dressed up, ye know. Get the kilt onto him. Bill's singing: 'I'm 94 this morn! 94 the day! I'm not so young as I used to be; I'm getting old and grey!' 'A bit jig, man, Bill! Give us a bit jig!' So Bill gives a bit dance. Whae, the long johns come down! And he got all bamboozled! O, dear me! That was the best part of the concert!

CD   *John Allan, Hector Hall and Bill Liddell at a concert, Beadnell, between the Wars. Before the days of television people made their own entertainments.*

Church

I don't think the fishermen here are as religious now as they used to be. One time, everybody used to go to Church, no question about that. That Church along there used to be fairly full, all the locals. But we haven't got many locals now – nowt but 'interloupers' as we call them! I was a choir-boy all my life, from being a little boy; went to Sunday School, Church morning and night, in the choir till just after the War when I finished. There used to be 20 men and 20 or 30 women in the choir here. Wartime knocked it on the head.

RW

Childhood

School: Barring-out Day

Oh aye, I went to the old school, up the stairs. Aye. And I'll tell ye something about that, now, that ye don't know anything at all about. They had what they called a lock-out day. Yes. And we used to get into the school first, before the schoolmaster. The schoolmaster lived down below, you see, and the school was on the top. And we used to get in first and tie the door, and he couldn't get in that day. That was what they called 'barring-out day'. The schoolmaster was not allowed in that school that day. But we had to stop all day! Every year, yes. Different days. The schoolmaster never knew what day it was going to be. Oh, no! He'd have had a long lie if he knew that. I was one of the culprits that used to tie the rope.

JH

Carra-paa'd

When I went to the school, they wouldn't allow you ever to use your left hand. Ye got the cane if ye used your left hand. O yes! So I write with my right hand, but I'm naturally left-handed. Carra-paa'd. That was the old name for a left-hander. 'O, he's carra-paa'd.'

Now, even after I started the sea, when ye were mending the net, ye had to use your right hand again. They wouldn't allow you to make a knot with your left hand. No. It's the wrong way. It had to be the right hand.

TDw

Games

We used to go and pick up what we called 'playgen' – any amount of folk'll not know what I'm talking about. Bits of pots, with the sea brushing on it back and forward, it rubbed the edges off until they were smooth. And we used to use them for lots of things. We played with them. Chucks – I never played chucks very much, but possibly they would use them for that and all. Little bits: they were bonny after the sea had rubbed them, blue and white and all sorts. We played with a lot of that. We fetched it up off the beach.

MF

A Girl at the Sea

When my mother died, Father used to take us to the sea with him, till I started school. When we got a house-keeper we were alright; but for that time, before he got a house-keeper, he wrapped us up and carried us down to the harbour; and he put us in under the green deck sheeting, on a cushion or a pillow; just me. Gladys was just a baby. Then we got a house-keeper. But I went with him a good few times. He used to say, I slept many hours at the sea. I used to come crawling out when it was stormy. I used to say, 'Look at this big'un coming!'

MF

Beadnell children at the Haven, circa 1927. Back row, left to right: Robbie, Stephen, and cousins Charlie 'Chuck' and Tom Douglas. Middle: Violet Douglas and Maggie Fawcus (with Gladys). Front: Rachel and Dorothy Baxter-Douglas, Percy Douglas and Mary Ann Stephens (grandmother).

Taking Stock

The small scale inshore fishermen of the Northumberland coast are more economically sustainable and less dependent upon technology than those who fish with bigger boats in deeper water. Relying upon knowledge which is handed down the generations, they have traditionally concerned themselves with both past and future. Conservation has always mattered to them: they want the fish to be there for their sons and grandsons. Ironically, they are also the first to suffer from the effects of over-fishing – and, still more, from the stranglehold of regulations designed to prevent it.

These regulations, which still apply around the country, mean that any fish caught which is undersize or outside the quota must be thrown back – dead. Thousands of tons of fish are unnecessarily wasted every year because of such absurd laws, made up by people who have little contact with the sea.

Seahouses, with its bigger harbour, acquired a fleet of small trawlers in the late 1960s. However, dwindling fish stocks and crippling regulations meant that this was short-lived, and most were sold off in the 1990s. In any case, Seahouses trawlers never fished on anything other than a small scale. As one Amble fisherman put it, 'if everybody was like the Seahouses men, and went off for only one day at a time, and stayed ashore at weekends, the government wouldn't need to worry about conservation.'

As fishing has declined, the holiday and leisure industries have grown to take its place as the economic mainstay of the coast. But, paradoxically, what attracts people to these villages is their unique identity, a sense of place formed by generations of fisher people. If fishing was to die out, there would be a danger that these villages could lose their individual character altogether.

Although Seahouses had a bigger fishing fleet than the other villages after the War, the men were still fishing on a relatively small scale. This photo of Seahouses harbour in the late 1940s includes, left to right, front row: BK 14 John Wesley, BK 40 the Blossom, BK 445 Nelsons. Second row: Faithful, Respect, Maginot. Third row: Cluaran, Sovereign. Back: Good Fellowship. Many of these names reflect Seahouses' strong Methodist tradition.

Over-fishing

It's the crabs that's worrying us now. Up here was a place where everybody used to come and catch crabs. Now (1991) we cannot get any on this ground. They used to get them regular, anything up to 80 stone. 30 to 40 stone was a regular catch. Often 50s and 60s. But now, we're pulling up 300 pots and plenty days not getting four stone out of them. It's horrible.

Since October I think about 80 quid has been the best pay we've had in one week. And it's been just around about the 20s and 30s. It's a grim situation for these young lads. They're lucky that there's some of them get a (fishing) party at the weekend. But it's a rough job; all the gear ye want is that expensive.

We used to fish all the crabbing grounds heavily for about three to four months and then leave them alone. The Beadnell men as well. Funnily enough, you always caught the males first, then the females last. I always knew when to leave, when you only got hens, and small. Then it was time to give the ground a rest. There was always a good fishing when we went back. That is not the case now. It is catch the last one if at all possible, and to hell with tomorrow.

These iron-framed lobster nets have done untold damage to the inshore grounds. Some boats leave them in all the time; and they wonder why there are no lobsters. They work up to 22 fleets of 30, hauling half each day. We all used to work eight to ten fleets and make a good living. I think I've had either 14 or 15 new cars and they all came out the North Sea! Go and ask them if they can do it now. No way could they.

I feel so badly about what is happening to our inshore fishing. How I wish I could do something about it. If something is not done quickly there are going to be no boats left. Take Seahouses: 84 men down to just a handful in a few years. Look at Beadnell and Craster. Boulmer is the same. This cannot go on, and I need not tell you what will be the outcome.

The 'Tinyen' Dawsons sorting fish, Seahouses 1950s. Left to right: Jimmy Donaldson, Bill Dawson, unknown, Charlie Dawson (white boots), Danny Allen. The Favourite is centre, the Faithful behind her.

Mending a herring drift net, Seahouses, late 1940s. Left to right: Jimmy Giloney, 'Dobbin' Robson and 'Bartie' Bertram. The new Speedwell BK 249 lies against the pier. Nets were dried on the dunes and on the site of the present golf course.

No one seems to care any more. The government could do something if they wished; but I don't think they care a rap what happens. They would rather close their eyes to what is happening, though they were glad of us in 1939-45, to save their hides and money.

Man has become too clever for his own good. He destroys everything he touches with his greed.

BS

When we was gaa'n to the net fishing in the *Cluaran* and the *Providence*, I carried the net below my arm. Now they've got to get a wagon to carry it. That's only greed. Well, it's ower-greedy men, ower-big boats and too big nets – that's what's done the fishing.

There's crab pots. 200, we worked, for three or four of us. Now they're working 400 for two. Greed again. I've told them that at the harbour and I've told them in Beadlin there. Well, they're catching as many lobsters – but it's the quantity of pots they've got in. 400 for two men. They're not thinking about anybody what's coming behind them.

But ye're talking small scale in places like this, ye know. If they wanted to keep the fishing right – I'm not talking about cobles and small boats, but what we call the white-fishing – haddocks, cod and all the likes of flat'uns: if they wanted to keep the fishing right, not just England, Scotland and Wales, but all other countries, they should've kept the boats to about 45 feet, so, when it came bad weather, ye had to come home. Now, they've got them 80, 90 and 100 foot, and when it comes bad weather they still gan out. There's no balance in it.

JW

We cannot blame anybody but ourselves. It's over-fished. In every way ye can think of, it's over-fished. Lobsters is over-fished. White fish is over-fished. We've done it ourselves. We're still doing it. They've introduced big boats. They've given people money to help them build great seine-net boats, which should never have been allowed. A (purse) seine-net is a massive net that encircles a whole shoal of fish. It'll enclose an area of fish as big as a football field; and every fish inside that net is caught. The bottom's pulled up, everything. Herring and mackerel they go for. Now they've cleaned up the mackerel down on the south coast – cleaned it altogether. They've cleaned the North Sea herring with the damn thing a few years back. It was in the *Fishing News* just last week: a purse-seiner found herring the other day so many mile off Peterhead. One vessel encircled that catch and filled three boats full of herring. And then they say, we haven't got no herring left. Where do they expect them to come from?

Well, the government was wrong years ago. This purse-seining carry-on – I think it was brought over from Holland or Norway. And they cleaned up their fishing. More or less wiped it out. And then the Scots boats said, that's the way to catch herring! We'll have some of them! Well, they got great massive grants, a million pound for a vessel, probably two now, they cost. And they'd get a big grant for these boats and the net and what have you; and the mackerel was more or less cleaned out. Now they're back at the herring again. And they'll wipe that out again.

There's none of that from Northumberland. It's the big ports that do it. But it's not a thing that should've ever been allowed. It should've been banned. It'll be stopped eventually. When the damage is done.

RW

Rules and Regulations

Ye see, our lot – they're only allowed a certain quantity of haddocks and cod. But the foreigners can load up. They take the small fish and everything. And

Two views from Dawsons' boat yard, Seahouses 1960. The yard closed in the 1990s. Today, no new cobles are built in Northumberland, and old ones are routinely destroyed to comply with the rules of decommissioning.

they get away with it. There's only one country put them right, and that was Iceland.

It's about finished, the way it's going on, I'm telling ye. Very bad. 'Cos there's no crabs, there's no lobsters, there's no fish nor nothing now; they've cleaned everything up. There's only one thing will bring the fishing around – another 10 or 12 year war, which ye divvin't want. Then there wouldn't be anybody to catch them, so they'd come around again. When we were very young it was bad, and a lot of them went away. They went to Blyth and Amble and different places, but they were no better off. Then the (First) War came, and the fishing come around again. It was alright. And that's what happened the last War and all.

And mind, ye know, Mr Government did it himself. They helped them buy boats, which is the wrong thing. Ye didn't have to be a fisherman. Anybody, Tom, Dick or Harry, gans and gets a boat and starts the sea. Mr Government gave them grants for to get the boats. They gave them the money for the boats, and now they're trying to cut them down again. Oh! They haven't a clue! If a man couldn't buy his own boat he shouldn't have been there.

Some of the boats now – two million for a boat! And then maybe 50 or 60 thousand for a great big purse net. Well, they're bound to clean everything up, aren't they? The size of the nets and one thing or another they have now. But there ye are. Fancy paying two million for a boat! I think I would rather just live on the two million!

O it's changed altogether. One time, ye were fishermen, ye practically did what ye liked. But now ye cannot. Ye cannot do what ye like now. Ye've even got to have a licence to fish in the quarry! What damn thing are ye going to get in the quarry? An old kettle or a pan! But ye have to have a licence. And mind, the ones that run the fishing – they haven't a clue. But they have good jobs, mind. They tell ye what to do.

It tells ye in the Bible that the fishermen were the Lord's chosen people; but not now, mind. Not now.

CD

Tourism and Development

I'm off the Parish Council, but I've been on over 25 years. My husband's uncle (Bill Douglas) had been chairman. And the year before he took ill, he asked me to go on. And I've been there ever since. Trying to keep the cars off the beach, that was our worst problem. And mind, we've fought against development, and we're still fighting against development. Ye see, that new estate (Longstone Close and Park, Beadnell) – how many will there be in there? About 200, maybe. Well mind, when they first built it, there was all hell broke loose – 1967, they started building them. They're mostly occupied now. There's not that many just summer houses. I don't know if it's come down, but at one time we had 70% summer houses. It's a short distance from Newcastle now. If ye had to go by bus, it's two and a half hours. But ye see, with the car, everybody's found every place out now.

MD

When August comes in, ye might as well not gan (trout fishing on the beach); because there's speedboats and motorbikes (jetskis). Do ye know what they said one day? A fella said, 'Ye've got to haul your gear, we're gaa'n water-skiing!' And we're trying to make a living!

CD

We're lucky in that we've got tourists. We've told them that we can't do without them and we're very glad to have them or we wouldn't have money for anything. The people in the village now, I tell them, we wouldn't even have them, if it wasn't that they had come on holiday and liked Beadnell and come to stay. And now they're like us – they say, 'O, roll on September!'

MD

Always Something Fresh to Learn

My old uncle that I went to sea with, he went with us after the War in the yawl for a time; and when he retired I says, 'Well, there's one thing – ye'll know all about it now.' He says, 'I was learning till the last day I was there.' And he was 95 when he died. There's always something fresh to learn about the sea.

AR

Most men who go fishing don't get a lot of money, but if you have your health it's a good job, and you don't have someone breathing down your neck all the time. It's healthy and the air is so fresh and clean, it's a pleasure to be alive. It is just great to go out and see the sea in its different moods. Fantastic!

BS

The Craster men's favourite stance on the hill overlooking the harbour.

Glossary of Technical Terms and Dialect Words

Dialect words are marked (d).

Ablow – below (d)
Airboxes – experimental floats fitted to some cobles by the RNLI
Article – animal with curly tail, unlucky to mention. See *guffy*

Baa'mskin – fisherman's oilskin apron (d)
Bailey – bailiff (d)
Bark – to preserve by tanning
Barrel – body of lobster
Bend – full strength of tide (d)
Bondager – female farm labourer
Brat – turbot (d)

Cheesecutter – peaked cap
Cleek – stick (d)
Cloot – cloth, rag (d)
Cran – 28 stone measure of herring
Creeve – crab or lobster pot (d)
Cutch – bark from Africa or Borneo, used to preserve ropes and nets

Darsay – dare say; an exclamation (d)
Dan – marker buoy
Dopper – oilskin (d)
Drak – to mop (d)
Drogue – sea anchor. Also *dreg* (d)

Farlins – trays for sorting herring
Fest'ners – rough bottom (d)
Fishrooms – space amidships in coble

Gerd, gerrard, gerrod – hoop (d)
Glass – weatherglass, barometer
Gliff – a shock (d)
Grape – garden fork (d)
Guffy – unlucky animal (d). See *article*

Hemmel – barn, usually arched (d)
Heuk – hook (d)
Hind – male farm labourer

Lempets – limpets (d)
Lint – main part of net

Maroon – rocket signal for lifeboat crew

Mash – mesh (d)
Messenger – rope attached to herring drift nets, holding fleet together
Mizzen – small sail used to keep boat's head into wind
Mule – double-ended boat

Netty – lavatory (d)

Pellet – small float (d)
Playgen – pottery (d)
Poke – sack (d)
Pull – to row

Ram plank – horizontal bottom plank of coble
Red – to untangle the line (d)
Rig – ridge (d)
Rippin' – jigging; fishing using unbaited hooks and shiny lead lure
Running net – part of salmon beach net running from shore

Scut – top upper plank at coble's stern (d)
Shuggy boat – boat-shaped fairground swing (d)
Skeyn – to shell bait (d)
Snood, sneyd (d) – finer line attaching hook to long line
Sollan – Solan goose, gannet (d)
Sprag – big codling
Stoothin' – plaster (d)
Swad – green weed; Holy Island – samphire (d)
Swull – basket used to hold line (d)

Tackety boots – studded boots (d)
Tath – feathery weed (d)
Teer (all the teer, all that e'er) – all that ever (d)
Thoft – thwart, seat in coble (d)
Thowelds – thole pins for oars (d)
Tow – rope (d)

Varnigh – nearly (d)

Yawl – keel boat
Yettlin – cauldron (d)